UBUNTU LINUX

Learn administration, networking, and development skills with the #1 Linux distribution!

Jerry Banfield

Nick Germaine

Publisher: *https://jerrybanfield.com/books*

COPYRIGHT

More Books by Jerry Banfield

https://jerrybanfield.com/books

TABLE OF CONTENTS

PREFACE

Thank you very much for reading this book! You are reading this now because you want to learn more about Facebook marketing and Facebook ads. I hope that I will answer all the questions you may have in the different chapters of this book and help you make the right choice for a strategy that will work for you to have success on Facebook.

VISIT
JERRYBANFIELD.COM

Get updates about Jerry Banfield's newest books and courses via email.

How did you get here with me?

In 2005 while I was in college at the *University of South Carolina*, I tried to start working online. I signed up for an *MLM* program and a survey website. A month later, I had refunds from both and figured working online was not possible because everything was a scam. The truth was I was afraid to fail again.

In 2011, I moved in with my wife and launched an online business focusing on video game addiction in an attempt to avoid dealing with any of my other problems. In a few months, I changed my business to selling T-shirts because I realized there was no money in video game addiction. A year after starting my business, I dropped out of my criminology *PHD* program at the *University of South Florida* to run my business full time, which by then had changed to helping clients with *Facebook* and *Google* ads based on my experience failing to do them successfully for myself.

In 2013, I started sharing everything I knew for free on *YouTube* because I hoped it would help me get more clients. By April 2014, I was nearly bankrupt after failing at *15+* different business models. I was also nearly dead from trying to drink the pain away and fortunately the fear of death motivated me to get into recovery. Being in recovery motivated me to focus more on being of true service to others and less on what I would get out of it. I started making courses online with *Udemy* which soon turned into my first real business. I partnered with as many talented instructors as I could and learned from top instructors how to get my courses the most sales.

In 2015, I tried making some inspirational videos sharing what I learned in recovery and got an amazing response on *YouTube*. To make the background on my videos more interesting, I started making the inspirational videos while playing video games. To make a more helpful website, I hired a freelancer to convert the videos into blog posts. A *Udemy* student named *Michel Gerard* then helped me turn those posts into books.

By 2016, the *Udemy* courses I was teaching had made nearly *2 million dollars* in sales with me receiving over *$600,000* of that. Things went so well on *Udemy* that they decided to launch a new pricing policy in April 2016 that reduced sales by *80%* site-wide which encouraged many instructors to leave. Since I did not take the hint, *Udemy* chose to ban me based on what they said were policy violations despite my best efforts to work within the rules.

Now I am trying out live streaming video games both for the self-help message and the hands on tutorials that I watch when I am playing a new game. Again I take another leap of faith in my business online which I hope is for the right reason of being in loving service here with you.

Thank you very much for reading this and I hope you enjoy the rest!

Jerry Banfield

Nick Germaine is a Udemy instructor. He is a Canadian software engineer, currently studying System Dynamics and IT through MIT. He's also a Linux administrator and manages VPS servers. He has been creating web-based software since 2005, desktop software since 2013, and managing Linux systems since 2012.

CHAPTER 1

Getting Started with Ubuntu Linux

Which to choose?

Introduction to Ubuntu Linux and Getting Started as a Power User

Together we are going take a journey through *Linux*. I plan to give you the knowledge you need to be a power user; but first we must ask the question: What is *Linux*?

Well, it depends on whom you ask. In order to understand *Linux*, we must go back in time.

In the early 1980s *Richard Stallman*, then working in the *AI* lab at *MIT*, started the *GNU* project with the goal of creating an entirely free and open *Unix*-like operating system. This all started when the lab got a new printer, but the license restricted his ability to modify the code. He had hacked earlier printers to electronically send messages to users who printed items when the printing was complete, as well as notifying other users when the printer was free to use.

By the early 1990s there was almost enough *GNU* software to create an entire operating system; however their kernel, the *GNU* Hurd, was not yet complete.

Meanwhile, in the early 1990s *Linus Torvalds* set out on a hobby project to develop a *Unix*-like kernel known as *Linux*. He used *GNU* software, such as *GNU's "C"* compiler, to do it. While a kernel on its own was useless, he ended up including *GNU* software with the kernel tree to release an operating system.

Later, *Richard Stallman's* free software foundation sponsored the group *Debian* to release a *GNU/Linux* distribution that was completely open for people to use and contribute.

Debian grew over the years from a small group of *Free Software Foundation* hackers, to the enormous community it is today. Due to its popularity, *Debian* has become the base of countless *Linux* distributions.

Because this is open software, anybody can read the source code, modify it, and then redistribute it. Because of this, we now have hundreds of distributions. It's kind of a mess, really. There are so many *Linux* distributions that a common problem for beginners is deciding which *Linux* distribution they should use.

While there are a few distributions out there that actually include their own software, one of the biggest problems in *Linux* is with how many distributions there are and the fact that a lot of them are the same. They may have new wallpaper and icons, while everything else is the same.

Ubuntu was started in the early 2000s and is owned and distributed by *Canonical*. The base of *Ubuntu* is *Debian*, and *Ubuntu* has become so popular that it has in turn been forked countless times. Forking is a process in which the operating system is used as the base of a new distribution.

Ubuntu includes its own desktop environment called *Unity* and has recently started distributing phones running a version of *Ubuntu*. *Canonical* also contributes bug fixes and other contributions upstream, meaning that they send these changes back to *Debian* to include in future releases. While

Debian releases new versions sporadically, *Ubuntu's* aim was to capture the stability of *Debian*, but release new versions more frequently. As such, *Canonical* releases two distributions a year, one in April and one in October. The naming convention of *Ubuntu* is year and month. So, the version we'll be using was released in October of 2015, and it's called *Ubuntu 15.10*. Every two years in April, a long-term support version called *LTS* is released and officially supported for five years, while releases between *LTS* versions are supported for only nine months.

Let's get started. To download *Ubuntu*, go to *http://www.ubuntu.com*. When the page loads, you'll see an option that says **Desktop** in the top navigation. If you're following along, we'll be working with that version for demonstration purposes.

Click on **Desktop**, and when you arrive on the **Overview** page, click **Download** *Ubuntu*; it's the big orange button in the main area. On the download page, you'll see a few versions.

If you will be running *Ubuntu* on a server, it makes sense to choose one of the long-term support versions, because you would only need to install a new version every five years. You can install more frequently, because there is a new *LTS* version every two years; but with a non-*LTS* version, there's only official support and bug fixes for nine months.

For now, I recommend you choose one of the nine-month cycles and download the latest stable release, which at the time of this publication is *Ubuntu 15.10*. You'll note that the *64* bit is recommended, and that's what you'll select if you are indeed running a *64*-bit processor.

You can either click the **Download** button to download it directly in the browser, or you can click *"Alternative downloads and torrents"* to view what other types of files you can download.

If you're running on a really super fast Internet connection, it doesn't really make a difference. The in-browser download is probably going to download just as quickly as a torrent; however, if you don't have an incredible Internet connection, a torrent download will make a lot of sense. A torrent download will download a lot quicker than it would in the browser.

You may not want to install *Ubuntu* directly onto your system at first. That's an awful big commitment to make when you you're not really familiar with the system. Instead, I recommend you download to a virtual machine, such as

VirtualBox.

Go to *https://www.virtualbox.org*. This is a piece of software that allows you to create virtualized machines. A virtual machine is a virtual computer, if you want to call it that. *VirtualBox* allows you to create different virtual machines, set them up differently, and start different operating systems on each one.

When you get to the *VirtualBox* home page, look for download options. *VirtualBox* offers different packages dependent on different operating systems.

You'll select the appropriate download version for your host machine. For example, if you are running *Windows 10*, select the *VirtualBox* version for *Windows* hosts. Click **the version** to start the download. Later, you'll learn how to install *Ubuntu* on a virtual machine using *VirtualBox*.

What are Linux Distributions?

Before we actually get into the installation and use of *Ubuntu*, we are first going to talk about distributions and what exactly that means.

You'll remember that *Debian* was one of the first major *Linux* distributions. Along with *Slackware*, *Red Hat*, and *openSUSE*, they are the four different types of *Linux* distributions. A type is categorized based on the package manager. There are different *Linux* distributions that are not based on these four, for instance, *Gen2* and *Arch Linux*; however, we're not going to focus on those at this time.

You'll recall that *Debian* started in the early 1990s, and as time went by it was forked, which means that other people came along and used the source code of *Debian* to create their own *Linux* distributions.

Ubuntu has also been forked many times. There are two different types of *Ubuntu* derivatives: those that are officially recognized and those that are not officially recognized. A few examples of officially recognized *Ubuntu* distributions are *Kubuntu*, *Ubuntu Studio*, *Lubuntu*, and *Xubuntu*. Basically, *Kubuntu* is *Ubuntu* with *KDE* preinstalled instead of *Unity*, which is the desktop environment of *Ubuntu*. We will go into more depth on desktop environments in future chapters.

Unity has a panel across the top of the screen with different indicators, a clock, and a user menu that allows you to access user accounts, system settings, etc. On the left side, *Unity* has another panel that acts as a dock. Opened applications and applications that you pin to the dock will appear here. At the top of the dock is a button used to launch the dash. The *Ubuntu* dash is incredible. I absolutely love it. While I don't like most things about *Ubuntu*, the dash is really awesome. You can actually search for files, programs, etc. You can even use the *Ubuntu* dash to find things online. It's actually a pretty great concept.

Kubuntu has *KDE* preinstalled, which is a different environment, so it will look and act differently. In *KDE5* the desktop environment is called *Plasma*, therefore *KDE Plasma 5*. You can see the differences. It has a list of open windows along the bottom of the interface, along with the indicators, time, and access to the main menu.

Kubunru, *Ubuntu Studio*, and others are officially recognized derivatives of *Ubuntu*, but *Linux Mint* is not. If you go to *https://linuxmint.com*, you'll see that they developed their own desktop environment called *Cinnamon*. The *Cinnamon* environment is beautiful, and it's one of my favorites. It's similar to a classic desktop environment in that it has a panel at the bottom with the main menu and a window list for open windows.

Elementary *OS* is another unofficial *Ubuntu* distribution for *Windows* and *OSX*. *Elementary* is fun to use. The aesthetics alone are mind blowing. It has the cleanest interface I've seen. There is a transparent panel at the top with an applications menu, a clock, and the indicators; and it's got a doc for open windows. Aside from their own desktop environment, they've also created other software specifically for use with *Elementary OS*, such as the *Pantheon* file manager. It's one of my favorite file managers because it does a lot of different things in really neat ways.

With *Ubuntu*-based distributions, installation is practically the same, with a few exceptions. Feel free to explore the different *Linux* distributions if you don't think you'll have problems following along as we learn how to install *Ubuntu*. When we get *Ubuntu* set up, we'll look at some configurations and changes. But for now, feel free to explore the vast ocean of *Linux* distributions.

In the next chapter we will learn how to install *VirtualBox* and *Ubuntu*.

CHAPTER 2

Installing Ubuntu in a Virtual Machine

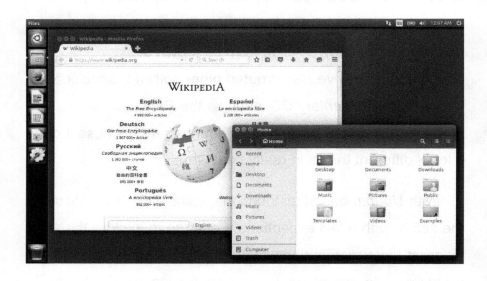

Installing VirtualBox and Setting Up Your Virtual Machine

In this chapter, you will learn how to install *VirtualBox* and then install *Ubuntu* in *VirtualBox*. You will use the files you downloaded in Chapter 1: the *VirtualBox* installer and the *Ubuntu ISO*, or disk image.

You'll start by running *VirtualBox* installer as administrator. Right-click the **VirtualBox installer** that you downloaded earlier, and then click **"Run as administrator"** from the window that pops up.

The installation is pretty straightforward. It doesn't require that you configure anything. Once it comes up, just click **Next**, **Next**, **Next**, **Yes**, and then **Install**. Once this installs, you'll see how you can create virtual machines, or virtual computers, that can run on your host, such as a *Windows* operating system. The virtual machines will have their own virtual disk images, which are basically like hard drives.

Once the installer finishes, leave the box checked that says, *"Start Oracle VM VirtualBox after installation"* because we want to start the *VirtualBox* immediately. Click **Finish** to complete installation and start the *VM*.

VirtualBox has a very clean and simple interface. You'll see a menu bar at the top, which you will probably never touch, and then a toolbar with icons.

To get started click **New** in the toolbar to create a new virtual machine. Let's name it *Ubuntu*. The type is *Linux*, and the version is defaulted to *Ubuntu (64-bit)*, which is great because we have a *64*-bit disk image of *Ubuntu* to use. Click **Next**.

Next, allot a certain amount of *RAM* for the virtual machine. You can set this to whatever you like, although typically you don't want this to go into the orange or pink field because that's going to give you less *RAM* on your host machine. I typically like to set it to about half my total *RAM*. You can enter the total *RAM* in *MB* for your computer in the box to the right of the *RAM* indicator.

Once you have set the *RAM* you want to allot to the *VM*, click **Next**. On the next screen, select *"Create a virtual hard disk now"*. For the Hard disk file type on the following screen, select *"VDI Virtual Disk Image"*. Click **Next**.

The following screen will ask you to select a storage type on the physical hard disk. You'll have the option to select **Dynamically** allocated or a **Fixed** size.

The difference between dynamically allocated and fixed size is that you'll be able to choose a target size for the *VirtualBox* disk image. With a fixed size, the size will always be the same. For example, if you set it to *20 GB*, the *VM* will always consume exactly *20 GB* on your host hard drive. If you dynamically allocate it, you can set the target size to *220 GB*, for example, but if there's only *5 GB* of actual data on the virtual drive, it will only consume *5 GB* on your host drive. It seems better to use dynamically allocated. Click **Next**.

Now, you can choose the target size of the hard drive. For example, if you want to allocate *20 GB* to the file size, use the slider to arrive at *20 GB*. Click **Create**. You now have a virtual machine, which will open automatically.

You now have an option to start immediately, which is indicated by the green arrow and **Start** icon. But this would be useless, because you have not yet told the *VM* what type of installation media you want to use. So, select the *VirtualBox* in the left menu and click **Settings**.

When the settings menu comes up, there's not much you need to do here; but you should go to **System** and make sure that, *"Enable I/O APIC"* and *"Hardware Clock in UTC Time"* are set as the defaults.

On the **Processor** tab of the **System** screen, you will see how much of your processor is being used. You can increase this, but I find you get worse performance the more cores you use. I don't recommend increasing the processor use.

Next, take a look at the **Acceleration** tab. Both options next to **Hardware Virtualization** should always be enabled. If you have trouble with this and you are on *Windows 10*, you'll need to take another step. Go into **Programs** and **Features** by right-clicking on the **Start** menu icon in *Windows*. Then click *"Turn Windows features on or off"*. Scroll down, and look for *Hyper-V* in the window that opens.

Hypervisor is virtualization technology that *Windows* includes by default. If it's checked, that means *Hyper-V* is pre-configured for use. If *Hyper-V* is unchecked, it is not configured for use. If you have trouble setting up a virtual machine, you should come to this window and make sure this is disabled. If it is checked and you uncheck it, you will be prompted to restart.

Once that is configured, go in to your *BIOS* and enable virtualization technology for your processor. To boot into the *BIOS*, restart your computer normally, and as soon as it comes back on, before you see the *Windows* logo, repeatedly strike the key, which is normally **F10**. Your motherboard might have a different key that it uses to get into the *BIOS*. Sometimes it is **F2**. Once you get into the *BIOS*, make sure *Virtualization Technology* is enabled. Just scroll down until you see this configuration.

Now, back to the *VirtualBox*. If you go to the **Display** panel in **Settings**, you will see that the video memory is set really low at *12 MB*. This won't help much, so move that all the way to the end, which is *128 MB*. Also, enable *3-D Acceleration*. *2-D Acceleration* is only available on *Windows* guest machines, therefore, it is irrelevant.

The **Storage** panel is where you will tell the virtual image to load your *Ubuntu ISO*. Select the **Empty** disk image, and then on the right side, under **Attributes**, you'll see an icon. Click **the icon** and select *"Choose Virtual Optical Disk File"*. Browse to where you saved the *Ubuntu* disk image or *ISO*. Select the *Ubuntu* disk image and click **Open**. This tells the virtual machine that you want to boot from this *ISO*. The **Empty** disk image under the **Storage** panel now shows your *Ubuntu* disk image as selected.

Click **OK**, and you can start the virtual machine.

It may take a little longer for *Ubuntu* to load in a virtual machine, as opposed to actually booting the *ISO* image on your hard drive. We will cover booting the *ISO* on your hard drive in another chapter.

Installing Ubuntu Linux on Your Virtual Machine

Ubuntu runs very minimalistic in *VirtualBox*. When loaded from your hard drive, it will look different. You may see a warning message when loading from a virtual machine, but it's not important, so just wait for it to load.

Once it does load, you may see scrollbars in the interface. You can scroll up and down, or left and right. You don't want that because it will make it difficult to navigate the machine. Go to **View** and select **Full Screen Mode**. In full screen mode, hover over the bottom of the screen and you get a menu that you can access. From this menu you can minimize, maximize, or close the screen.

When loading the installation you can try it first, or you can install it straight to the disk, or in this case, the virtual disk. Click **Install** *Ubuntu*.

You can also download updates and third-party software during initial installation. If you're using this on your personal machine and not a server, you probably want the third-party software because this allows you to play *MP3* files, *MP4* videos, and a host of other file formats that it will recognize with proprietary third-party software. When you've finished selecting installation options, click **Continue**.

The next step asks if you want to erase disk and install *Ubuntu*. Because we're running in a virtual machine, it is safe to do so. It will not erase your entire hard drive. Instead it will use the *20 GB* of virtual hard drive space that you predefined in previous steps. However, let's look at partitioning for a moment. We'll be diving into this later, but for right now, it's good to have a bit of knowledge.

Select **Something Else** from the **Installation Type** screen and click **Continue**. You'll see your virtual disk drive displayed on the next screen. It's called *SDA*. You need to **Create** a **New Partition Table**, because it's a fresh hard drive. When you see the message *"Create a new empty partition table on this device?"* click **Continue**. Now you have *21,000 MB* of free space. You are going to create a partition, which is going to serve as the swap area. Swap space is like extra *RAM*.

Click on your **free space**, and then click the plus sign on the *"+ or - Change"* button below. Under the **"Use as"** option, select **"swap area"** and change the size to about *5 GB*.

Swap space serves as sort of extra random access memory that is not on the *RAM*, but it's actually on the hard drive. It's a bit slower than *RAM* and uses it for different reasons, and it's necessary. On an actual installation, I like to set that to about *8* to *16 GB*, but because we're working with limited space here, we can make it *5 GB*.

Once you create a swap area, you're going to see that the free space is now listed. You have *16 GB* left, so click the **free space** and the **plus sign** again, and this time use as *"Ext4 journalizing file system"*. That's the file system type. If you use the drop down, you'll see that there are others. This is the best option to choose when running *Linux*. It's really fast.

For the mount point, set it to forward slash *"/"*. This will tell the installation that you want to use this partition that you are now creating, the *16 GB* partition, as the entire file system. In *Linux*, *"/"* represents the route. If you wanted to send this to your home partition, which is a specific partition for user files, you could type *"/home"*, reduce that size, and then use another partition for the **Route**. We will get into that more later.

Go ahead and install everything to this partition, and click **OK**.

We won't touch *"Device for boot loader installation"*. *Ubuntu* is pretty smart at determining where to install the boot loader. You are installing in *Legacy* mode, not *EFI*, which is an awesome technology to use when dual booting multiple operating systems; but for this demonstration in *VirtualBox*, you've only got one.

Setting Up Ubuntu Linux on Your Virtual Machine

Now you're going to set up *Ubuntu*. Choose your time zone and click **Continue**. Select your keyboard layout. *English US* should be fine for most; however, if you have an alternative keyboard layout, you should choose the correct one, otherwise the keys will not be correctly mapped. You can use the test feature in *Ubuntu* on this screen. You can also select to **Detect Keyboard Layout**.

Once you've chosen the correct keyboard layout, click **Continue**.

Let's set up a user. Your computer's name can be anything you want. It's simply a way to identify your machine, both in computer language and if you're looking, for instance, on your router and you're trying to see which machines are connected. In that case, the computer's name will be shown. Enter a **username** and **password**. You'll see some extra options: **Log in automatically** or **Require my password to log in**. Obviously, log in with a password is more secure. Once you've made your choices, click **Continue**.

Next you'll be presented with the *Ubuntu* **Welcome screen** and a demonstration of what to expect with *Ubuntu*. Use the icons to scroll left and right through the demo.

You'll see a demo of the **Software Center,** where you can install, uninstall and manage software on your computer. You'll also see that *Ubuntu* comes with *Rhythm box* music player, which is great. It also comes with *GIMP*, which is image software. You can install *GIMP*; it is not preinstalled. *GIMP* is an open source alternative to *Photoshop*. You'll also find video editors. *Firefox* is preinstalled. You can install *Chromium* and *Flash*. *Chromium* is an open-source version of *Google Chrome*. You can install *Google Chrome*; we will go through that in another chapter.

LibreOffice is preinstalled. If you don't want to use this, *WPS Office* is a great alternative, but it doesn't use the *ODT* format.

The next demo shows how you can customize your machine. You can set the background. Obviously that's a feature you would expect from any operating system. You can also make other configurations, but we will get into those shortly.

You can also get support with *Ubuntu*, which has many great options for asking questions and reporting bugs. There are bugs; you'll probably not encounter any, or if you do, they should be small and won't really have much impact on you. You'll also note there are some links that you can go to once you reboot into the *Ubuntu* operating system. Again, this is just an installer.

Once *Ubuntu* has successfully installed, you can select **Restart Now**. You'll also want to select your **current disk**. Hover over the menu bar at the bottom of the installer screen. Select **Optical Drives**, and then uncheck the *Ubuntu* **disk**.

Once your computer restarts, it should take you into the *Ubuntu* system.

Disabling the ISO & First Boot Up

If for some reason your virtual machine locks up and there's a warning message, use the window controls to close it. Hopefully you won't have this issue, but if you do, you want to make sure that once you shut down and restart, your computer will not try to boot up using the same *ISO*, because we no longer need this *ISO* to install it.

Make sure in **Storage Controller**: *IDE* is **Empty**, and go into the drop down menu to the right, next to **Optical Drive**, and make sure *Ubuntu* is unchecked. If checked, just click it to uncheck it. Click **OK**.

Now you can start the virtual machine. Just click **Start**. It should be exactly the same as the previous boot process. You'll see the *Ubuntu* loading screen.

Once *Ubuntu* loads, use the same process as before. Click **View** in the *Ubuntu* menu bar at the top left, and go to **Full-screen Mode**. You can also use a shortcut by clicking the **right control key and F.**

Next, you'll see **Light DM**. This is the login screen manager for *Ubuntu*. You'll enter your **Username** and **Password** and hit **Enter**. The first screen after login displays a list of keyboard shortcuts. The most notable thing here is that the **Super** key, which opens the **Launcher**. It is also called the *Windows* key and is located on your computer keyboard to the left of the spacebar. It has a *Windows* icon. That is the *Super* key.

In the next chapter, we will go through a basic configuration of the system.

Jerry Banfield & Nick Germaine

CHAPTER 3

Optimizing Ubuntu & Customizing Your Desktop

Installing VirtualBox/Guest Additions for a Better User Experience

In this chapter, we will look at how to set up *Ubuntu* and perform some basic configurations for the system.

First, you need to install a virtual box component called *Guest Additions*. This allows you to run the virtual machine in a more stable environment and with higher performance.

Hover over the menu bar on the bottom of the screen, select **Devices**, and then **Insert Guest Additions CD image**. When you get a message that says you are unable to insert the virtual optical disk *C*, click the **CD** icon at the bottom left of the *Ubuntu* icon task bar. This opens the optical disk.

As you can see, the performance is terrible, so right-click the icon for **VBoxLinuxAdditions.run**, select **Properties** from the popup menu, and make sure that it is executable. In the **Properties** window, make sure the box is checked for *"Allow executing file as program"*.

Now, let's go into **Terminal**, or command line, for a moment. This will be your first look at **Terminal**. We will cover quite a bit of the command line interface in *Linux* later. It's quite powerful.

Click the **Super key**, which will bring up the *Ubuntu* dash. You can also click the icon on the top left of the *Ubuntu* file manager to bring up the dash.

You'll see different scopes at the bottom of the screen. *Ubuntu* will load in the default *Home* scope, but you want to switch to *Applications*, and you'll see *Installed*, *Recently Used* and *Dash* plugins. Select **Installed** so you can look at the applications that are installed on the system. This is pretty inefficient if you're trying to launch an application and know exactly which application you want to load. Instead, click the **Super key** bringing up the dash again, and start typing the application name that you want to run, in this case **Terminal**. You can see once you start typing *"term"*, the first result is **Terminal**. This is the one you want to launch. If the application you're searching is the first in the list, you can just hit **Enter**, and it should launch that application.

There are shortcuts in *Linux* to launch **Terminal**, and one of them is to click *CTRL*, *ALT*, and *T* on your keyboard at the same time. It will bring up *Terminal*.

You'll need to open to a specific location in *Terminal*. Instead of opening within *Applications*, go back to the file manager of *Ubuntu*, right-click, and select **Open in Terminal**. You'll see the location *VBOXADDITIONS* in the *Terminal* window.

Run this program:

```
sudo ./VBoxLinuxAddtions.run
```

It must be run with administrative privileges, which means you need to add sudo to the beginning of this command.

The great thing about *Linux* is that for anything to actually modify the core of the system, install applications, or remove them, administrator rights are required. You will also be forced to enter a password. This can get frustrating sometimes and there are ways around it, which we will discuss later.

Run files, or files with *.run* file extensions, can be run directly from *Terminal* by typing the name of the file and **.run**. You'll also want to add **"."** and **"/"** to indicate to *Terminal* that the file you want to run is in the current directory. So, **"./"** in Linux means current directory. This tells *Terminal* that the file is in the current directory and the run extension says automatically run the file. You don't really need to know how to issue a ton of commands, but running files is pretty simple.

The *Terminal* will add kernel modules. The kernel, as we discovered in chapter 1, is called *Linux*, which is the kernel for *Ubuntu*, *Debian*, *Fedora*, and every other distribution out there that uses *Linux* as the kernel. The kernel's job is to translate between software and hardware. Right now, you have a screen with terrible resolution. Perhaps it's *1280 x 768*, so it's very square; not a wide screen. By installing this module, you'll be able to configure the screen resolution to a resolution that the hardware actually supports. That's why you need to install *VirtualBox Guest Additions,* in order to get better performance. The system will also be very laggy, but you should see a huge increase in performance once you reboot after installing *VirtualBox Additions*.

Now you can restart *Ubuntu*, and hopefully you'll have better screen resolution and less lag. To restart, close **Terminal**, and in the *Ubuntu* file manager, click the **gear icon** in the upper right corner, click **Shut Down**, and then **Restart**.

Customizing Your Ubuntu Desktop

The first notable thing you'll see once restarting *Ubuntu* with *Guest Additions* installed is that the resolution is now correct. It's running at *1366 x 768* pixels, which is exactly what you want.

Enter your **password** and hit **Enter** to reload *Ubuntu*. Now you should see some speed and better performance. Try opening the dash. You should see less lag.

Let's get started with customization. The dash with the *Launcher* on the left-hand side already has some items pinned to it. If you don't want something pinned, you can simply right-click and select **Unlock from Launcher.** If you want to move stuff around, you can hold your left mouse button until it slightly displaces the item, and then you can move it up or down and pin it wherever you want.

In order to get the new configurations, you need to download some files. Open *Firefox*. You'll be looking for a theme and an icon theme.

What is a theme in *Linux*? *Unity* is the desktop environment you are currently using, and it uses the *GTK* theme. The *GTK* theme controls everything about how things look. For example, the way your window controls appear, the dark gray title bar, and the way the selected color is orange, are all due to the theme. These are all things you can change, but in order to do so, you need some *GTK* themes. You can get those by going to *http://gnome-look.org.*

Older *GTK* themes may break with your current version of *Ubuntu*, so scroll down to the download links for each theme and make sure it's compatible with your *GTK* version. Feel free to explore all of the themes. You can click the images of the themes to enlarge them and see what they look like.

Once you have selected a theme for download, you can choose to either save the downloaded file or open it. For now, open it in **Archive Manager** and **Extract**. This will open a file browser, and you can choose where you want to extract the installer. Once it's done extracting, you can leave the archive manager open, or you can quit. Go ahead and quit for now.

You'll also need an icon theme. There are some similar issues with icon themes as there are with **GTK** themes for different versions of **GTK**. Some icon themes don't appear to have every necessary icon, so they can look a bit messy. Click on **the images**, which will make them larger, to get an idea for how the icons look. Once you've selected an icon theme, download it. Icon themes are typically a lot larger than **GTK** themes. I've seen archives as large as *300 MB*. That's quite large.

You'll also want to open and extract the icon themes files with an archive manager once it has finished downloading.

While your icon themes are downloading, you can search for a nice wallpaper. Do a *Google* search for wallpaper images. Use the *Google Images* tab to view thumbnails of the images *Google* returns. Scroll through the images and find one you like. Once you find a wallpaper you like, enlarge it by clicking on it. Then right-click on the **enlarged image** and select **Save Image As**, and choose where to save it.

Next, you're going to install an application to really help you configure your system. You could go to the **System**

Settings, which are located under the gear icon in the upper-right in *Ubuntu*. This is good for some things, but there is actually a tool designed to give you more control over your system. In the system settings you can change the appearance of the system minimally. You can change the wallpaper and the size of the icons on the left. System settings has a behavior tab too. You can auto hide the launcher if you choose. You can get great control over the mouse and power settings, and you can change the screen display for the correct resolution. There are also sound settings and some other things to explore. But you want more customization that this.

Installing the Unity Tweak Tool for Ubuntu

Let's install something called the *Tweak Tool*. This tool will allow you to better configure the system.

Bring up **Terminal**. Remember, you can use *CTRL ALT T*. Run another task as administrator, which means you need to type *sudo*. You can use a program called *"apt-get"*, which allows you to manage software either by installing or uninstalling. The action you'll want to use is **"install"**, and the program you want it to install is called **Unity Tweak Tool**. This is what you will type in *Terminal*:

```
sudo apt-get install unity-tweak-tool
```

Once you type a command in Terminal, you hit **Enter** to run the command. Next, type your **password**. When you type your **password** into *Terminal*, you'll never see the letters being typed, but they are indeed being entered. *Unity Tweak Tool* will now be installed.

Go to the folder where you saved the theme and icons files that you downloaded earlier. These are the actual directories, and if you open them you should see other files, including index files. Select all of these files and copy them. In the *Ubuntu* file manager, you can click **CTRL T** to open a new tab. In the new tab, go to **Home**. You won't be able to see the hidden directories, so click **CTRL H** to see all of the hidden files and directories. Any file or directory that begins with a "." is denoted as a hidden location, or hidden file. You need to create one of these for themes, so right-click and select **New Folder**. Name it *".themes"* and hit **Enter**. Then, in this themes directory, paste the themes that you selected from the other tab.

You need to do the same for the icons. Copy all of the files in the icon directory, open another tab and create a hidden directory called "**.icons**". Paste in the copied files.

Now you have the *Unity Tweak Tool* installed, and the themes and icons are located in the new directory.

Open up the dash and type **Tweak** in the search bar. If you can't find it, it could be because you recently installed it. Sometimes *Ubuntu* doesn't register changes immediately in the dash. Keep this in mind.

While you are waiting for *Ubuntu* to recognize the new files, let's take this opportunity to talk about how a file system works. If you go to your computer's hard drive, this is the root directory, as explained previously. Your *User* directory is in *Home*. You'll notice "**/user**" shows up frequently in the system. Bin in the *User* directory contains binary files that you can run, but you wouldn't typically run them by navigating to the *Bin* directory.

Back in the *User* folder, *Share* is the shared directory, which is basically used as a place to house configuration files for binary applications. You also have an *Applications* directory, which has all of the installed applications. These are all **.desktop** files. You can't see the file extension, but that's what they are. Basically, when you run one of these or open them from the dash, these files contain information about what binary files to run, from where, how, etc.

Let's change the desktop wallpaper. It's simple. Find an image file on your system. You can choose the one you selected earlier or choose another. Right-click on **the image** and select **Set As Wallpaper**. Easy, right?

By now, the *Unity Tweak Tool* should be installed. Double-click it to launch the **Tweak tool**. This is what you will use to customize the system.

Let's change some things about the *Launcher*. Click **Launcher** in the menu of the *Unity Tweak Tool*. You can set it to auto hide, but don't do that just yet. You can also change the icon size. For example, you can take it down to *38* pixels and make it a bit more transparent by using the slider. You can also change it to a custom color, rather than a color based on the wallpaper. If you turn transparency all the way down, you can see what color was actually chosen.

Click **Panel** in the menu. You can also change the panel by making it entirely transparent, sort of transparent, or not transparent at all, using the slider. This should depend on the theme you will be using.

Click back to **Overview** at the top of the *Unity Tweak Tool* window. Under **Appearance**, select **Theme**. If *Theme* doesn't appear to be working, try this:

Go to the **Home directory**, open the *".themes"* folder, and select the theme you are using. Here's the problem: You may have your actual theme folder inside another general themes folder. You need to place the actual themes folder directly into the *".themes"* folder. You can drag and drop it to the correct *"themes"* location.

Restart **Unity Tweak Tool**. Go to your computer's hard drive and follow the path: ***User/Share/Applications*** and find **Unity Tweak Tool**. Once it launches you can select the theme you want to use.

Over in **Icons**, select the icon theme that you downloaded. You can also go into the **Cursor menu** and customize the cursor. In *Window Controls,* you can make some selections to the *Layout*. For example, you can choose to have the icons on the left or right, and you can choose whether or not to show the menu button. You can go back to the **Panel Settings** and change the transparency.

Now you have a customized version of *Ubuntu*. Feel free to explore customization more and do any configurations you would like.

In the next chapter, we will be talking about desktop environments. The desktop environment you are currently using is *Unity*, albeit a slightly customized version of *Unity*.

CHAPTER 4

Installing Ubuntu

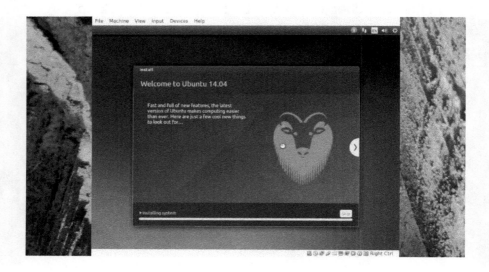

Installing Ubuntu Alongside Windows on Your Hard Drive

In this chapter you will learn how to install *Ubuntu* alongside your *Windows* installation on your actual hard drive. You will need a few things for this installation. First, you will need a *USB* drive. I recommend *8 GB* or larger. You also need a program called **uNetbootin** from *www.unetbootin.sourceforge.net*. Download the *Windows* version.

Plug the *USB* drive into your computer, and then, right-click on the **Windows Start menu** icon at the lower left-hand portion of your screen. This should be the same for every version of *Windows* since *Windows XP*. When you right-click on the **Start** icon, you will get a menu. Find **Disk Management** and click on it. You're going to format the *USB* drive so that you can install the *ISO* image of *Ubuntu* on it. You'll recall that you already downloaded the *Ubuntu ISO* image and saved it to your computer.

Take a look at the **Disk Management** screen. If you've never formatted the hard drive, you will probably see a few smaller partitions at the beginning of your hard disk, and then a very large *C: drive*, which should be in *NTFS*. That is your *Windows* partition.

Find your *USB* drive. It should be labeled **Removable**. Right-click on it, and select **Format**. You can name it anything you like. The important thing is that the file system must be *FAT32* in order to boot from that *USB* drive. I recommend checking *"Perform a quick format"*, otherwise it will take a while. Once that is selected, leave everything else alone, and click **OK**.

Your drive should format pretty quickly. Once it has finished formatting, remove it from the *USB* port on your computer, and then put it back in. This will mount it so that *uNetbootin* can see it, and so you can install it. When you plug the *USB* drive back into your computer, it should recognize the *F drive*; if not, select the **F drive**.

In the *UNetbootin* screen, you will need to select the **Ubuntu Disk image** that you downloaded earlier, which you will burn to the *USB* drive. Select the **Disk image** radio button, select *ISO* in the drop down menu, if it is not the default, and browse to the **Ubuntu ISO image**. This is the same image you installed in *VirtualBox*, and now you will use it to install *Ubuntu* alongside your *Windows* operating system.

Make sure you select **USB Drive** for the *Type* and the appropriate *USB* drive in the *UNetbootin* window; it should read **"F:"**. Click **OK**. The *ISO* image will burn to the *USB* drive.

Next, you will be prompted to reboot or exit. It's important to do one thing before you reboot your computer. *Windows* has a feature called fast startup, which will interfere with your ability to access the *Windows* drive. You will need to repartition the *Windows* drive so you can get access to

Windows from *Ubuntu*.

Here's how fast startup works: basically, when you shut down your computer normally, your computer doesn't fully shut down. There still things running. It's like hibernation. So you need to change how that works. Right-click on **your battery icon** on the lower right-hand portion of the *Windows* screen, and select **Power Options**.

On the left-hand side, click *"Choose what the power button does"*, and then on the next screen click *"Change settings that are currently unavailable"*. This will allow you to change the **Shutdown settings** on the following screen. Uncheck the box that says, *"Turn on fast startup"*. Click *"Save changes"*. Now, you may either reboot, or exit and manually restart your computer.

Reboot Your Computer Using Ubuntu

In this section you will learn how to reboot your computer using *Ubuntu* as the operating system.

When your computer is turned off and you want to start it again and reboot with *Ubuntu*, you will need to press the key to enter the *BIOS* boot menu. Remember that earlier I told you this is usually the **F10** key on the *PC* but it could be different on your computer. Make sure you tap this key while the computer is rebooting. There is a very limited window of time in which this key needs to be pressed to reboot into *Ubuntu*.

If you are on an *EFI* system, make sure you choose the **USB Hard Drive *(UEFI)***, and then hit **Enter**. Use your up-and-down keys to select the correct device, and then hit **Enter**. This will allow you to boot off the hard disk. Click **"Try Ubuntu"** on start up. The boot up process should be relatively quick.

You're now booted into *Ubuntu*. Double-click the **Install Ubuntu** icon on the desktop. When it opens, select your language, and click **Continue**.

You will want to connect to a wifi network, unless you are connected through ethernet. This is necessary so that you can download updates while installing. You want to get fresh packages from the repositories.

You will then see these big check marks telling you that you're all good to go. Also, check ***"Download updates while installing"*** and ***"Install this third-party software"***. You don't really need to install third-party software, but this allows you to play *MP3* files and other proprietary file types. When you're ready, click **Continue**. The installer will now begin scanning your hard drive.

Next, you will see a screen that prompts you to install *Ubuntu* alongside *Windows*. Don't do that, because you're going to manage the partitions manually, and that will give you a little more control. Select *"Something else"* at the bottom and click **Continue**. The hard drive will be scanned again, and this time you will see a different screen.

You should now see your windows partition in the list on the screen. You can find the *Windows* partition because it's formatted as *NTFS* and also by the size of the drive, which is rather large. You'll also see your free space.

The *NTFS* file system is the *EFI* partition. You are going to focus on the *Windows* partition right now. You will need to shrink the *Windows* partition in order to get more free space.

Click on the **NTFS partition**, and click **Change** at the bottom, using the **+ and - selections**. Reduce the size of this partition. *Windows* does take up quite a bit of space, along with the applications running on it, so I recommend leaving this relatively high. I have about *500 GB* that I use for my *Windows* partition and that's plenty. Once you've done this, click **OK**, and you will see another hard drive rescan. It will show you that you now have free space.

Next, you need to set up a few new partitions. Click **the free space** and click **the +**.

The first partition you will create is a swap area, which acts sort of like *RAM*, as you will recall; but this time we will create it on the hard disk. For the size of the swap area, use **the +** to change the partition so that it has about double the amount of *RAM* that you have. Make sure **Use as:** is set to **swap area**. Click **OK**. When it refreshes you will see the swap area you just created, followed by the free space.

Now you can create your main partition of the installation of *Ubuntu*. Select **free space**, and use the **Change +** to add a partition.

For **Use as:** select *"Ext4 journaling file system"* and set the **Mount point** to a *"/"*, and then click **OK**. Basically, the forward slash just indicates your entire operating system. The home directories, applications, and configurations will all be installed to this partition.

Linux gives you a bit more flexibility that we will not go into right now, but you are able to create two different partitions. One for *"/"*, the main partition, and another in which you can set the **Mount point** to **/home**. This will mean that all your user directories are stored on this partition. This makes sense for upgrading and installing different versions of *Linux*, because the home directory will always remain intact, and you won't need to format every time you installed *Linux*. You can install the next over the root partition.

Now your partition is set and you are good to go.

The device for the boot loader is important. If you are not running in *EFI* system, you need to leave this to **dev/sda**. This means the boot loader is going to be written to the very first sectors of the hard disk, which is where *non-EFI* hard drives store their boot loaders with *Windows*. It will replace the *Windows* boot loader with *GRUB*, which is a *Linux* boot loader. It will also give you an option during installation for the boot loader to boot into *Windows*. Every time you boot up your computer, you will see *Boot* into *Windows* or *Boot* into *Linux*. Every computer released in the last few years is an *EFI*, and *EFI* is great. It allows you to better manage dual or tri-boot installations or operating systems on your hard disk.

You will install the *EFI* files for the boot loader on the existing *EFI* partition, which is **sda2**. When you are ready, you can click **Install Now**. You will receive a message that the *"install"* will make these changes, they are permanent, and you may lose data if you've done something wrong, so please make sure you do this correctly. This will leave your *Windows* partition intact because you are not formatting the partition, you are just shrinking it and creating some new partitions.

After you review these changes, click **Continue**, and the *Ubuntu* operating system will be installed on your hard disk. The installation procedure is exactly the same as it was in *VirtualBox*. Choose your location and time zone and select your keyboard layout. Next, create your **user account** with a **username** and **password**. You have a few options, including to log in automatically or require a password. Click **Continue**, and you will be presented with this beautiful slideshow of everything *Ubuntu* can do. Well, not everything, but a few things. We will dive into more of these things later.

You will receive a message when the installation has been successfully completed, and now you're free to either continue testing on the *USB* drive or to restart. If you plan to continue testing, click the **reboot button**, the **gear icon**, in the top right-hand corner, when you are ready to shut down.

CHAPTER 5

Getting Started with the Linux Command Line

In this chapter we will finally get to the command line, and I'm really excited about this because this is probably the key aspect of *Linux* you will need to learn. It's great to have a bit of background knowledge and to learn how to install the system, but those are very small and insignificant in comparison to how much you'll be working with command line.

To open up the command line you will use a program called *Terminal*. You can access this in the *Applications* menu by typing *Terminal*, or you can use *CTRL, ALT "T"* on your keyboard.

We are going to talk about a few commands for now. The first one is *"pwd"*, which **prints the working directory**. If you type *pwd* in *Terminal*, it will list the current directory, for example */home/user*. This is your user directory and the default location.

The second command we will explore is *"cd"*, or **change directory**. This allows you to change the directory in which you are working. For example, you can type ***cd /user/share***, and it will take you to the */user/share* directory. When you are changing directories, if the first character after *cd* is a forward slash, that means it will be an absolute path from the beginning of the hard disk, or from the root directory. You could *cd* into your home directory by typing ***/home***.

So how do you change directory with a relative path? You just omit the *"/"*, and this will tell *Terminal* to change from your current directory and take you to the next level.

Linux also uses *"./"* to indicate the current directory. This means you will stay in the same directory. For example, you can type **cd ./lib** and that will take you to the directory called *lib*, which is located in your current directory.

Let's say you wanted to go to a directory called username nick. You could type it like this: **cd /home/nick**

But if you were feeling really lazy, you could use "~", which you will find left of the number 1 on your keyboard and directly under the *ESC* key. You can access the symbol by holding down the shift key. This symbol means home, and it will take you to your */home* directory, which is unique for each user.

We can use the symbol and put a different spin on it. Let's say you are in */user/share/applications*. You can type **pwd** to see your current directory. If you want to go directly to *home/nick*, you can type **cd ~**, but if you want to go to *home/nick/documents*, you can use **~/documents**.

This is all fun, but what's the point of navigating a file system if you really can't do anything? Next, we will learn a command that will help us do something.

Start in the */home* directory. Let's say you want to go up a level. Remember how changing directory with "./" means current directory? If you use "../" you can go up one level to the parent directory. For example, if you are in *home/nick* and type *"../"* and then hit **Enter**, you will go to the */home* directory. You can type *pwd* to see that you are in the *home directory*.

Did you get this?

Move to home directory: **cd~**

Move to current directory followed by a relative path: *./*

Root of the directory with absolute path: *I*

Go up one level: *../*

Go to your */home* directory. The next command is *"ls"*, which lists the contents of the current directory. For example, in your home directory you can type *"ls"* and see a list of all of the files and folders in your home directory in alphabetical order.

The *ls* command is a big command. There are many options you can throw at it, but we are going to focus on just a few.

File permissions in *Linux* are very important. They define who can do what and to which files. For instance, the *a.out* file is a binary file from a *C++* program written by a developer, and it belongs to him. That means he can run it. But how do we know that it belongs to him? We can use the *ls* command separated by a space, dash, and the letter **"l"**. It looks like this in command line: *ls -l*

The -l argument gives you a list that is in a longer format and with additional information. In the left column, the information listed shows the permissions of a file by *owner*, *user* and *group*.

So, *"ls -l"* lists permissions. It lists the *owner's* user account and also the corresponding *group*. When you create a *user* in *Linux*, it also creates a *group*, at least during the main installation, and the *group's* name is the same as the username. The *"ls -l"* command also shows the date modified and some other information. What if you wanted to list a directory based on some other things?

You can list the contents of a directory in reverse order: *ls -r*

You can define file types in a list: *ls -p.*

You can see that the directory is followed by the slash: *"/"*

You can also sort based on file size: *ls -s*

The items in the list are also color-coded. Directories are generally blue and other files are generally white, but the *a.out* file is a binary file, so it is green.

What we've been doing so far is listing contents of the current directory. Now, that's cool, because if you wanted to see every file that was in the */applications directory*, you would change directory to *user/share/applications*, and once there, you would type *"ls"*. This would show you all of the files and directories within this path.

Now, this works, but let's say you didn't want to leave your home directory, but you did want to list the files in the */ applications directory*. You can pass an argument after **ls** for the path you want to list: *ls /user/share/applications.*

Here's a bonus command for *Terminal*. The **"clear"** command makes *Terminal* a little less cluttered.

If you want to list files in */home/documents*: *ls ~/* ***Documents***

Let's say you wanted to list them in reverse order. You could do that: *ls ~/Documents*

You can start stringing commands together, at least the **ls** command, and if you're ever really lazy and don't want to type the entire **ls**, you can just type *"l"*.

Change directory: ***cd***

Print the current directory: ***pwd***

List the contents of a directory: ***ls***

For more options for the ***ls*** command, as well as an explanation of what they do: ***ls --help***

Administrative privileges in the Linux Terminal

I mentioned file permissions briefly in the previous section. We didn't really jump in, so I propose the scenario where I have created a file in a location to which I don't have access. Let's suppose I created the file ***"etc"***. It's in the */etc* directory, and it's just called *"file"*.

If you change directory to */etc* and then type *"l"*, you would see the contents of the */etc* directory. Let's say you want to edit this newly created file. You will use *nano* to edit this file. We will go into *nano* more later. *Nano* is a *Terminal* application for text editing.

Open the file: **nano ./file**

That's great. You can open it. But what happens when you try to write to it?

If you use *CTRL O* on your keyboard, which is the command to save this file, and hit **Enter**, *Terminal* will return an error, warning that you don't have permission to write to this file. If you use *CTRL X* on your keyboard, it will ask you if you want to save changes, and you can say *no*, because you can't. Well then, how do you edit that file?

You need to use administrator privileges in order to be able to edit a file for which you don't have permissions. There're two ways to do this.

The first one is to type *"sudo"* before the command, which is an abbreviation for *"super user do"*. It is a term in *Linux* that identifies your privilege level. So, *sudo* allows you to make changes to files and performs administrative tasks for this one command.

Try it:

```
sudo nano ./file
```

Now you can edit the file. Try to write a line to the file:

```
test343
```

Use *CTRL O* and hit **Enter**. Success. You will see a message that says you wrote 1 line. Now you can exit and your changes will be saved.

What if you don't want to retype the entire command?

Try it:

```
nano ./file
```

If you try to write to the file, it will fail because permission is denied. You haven't run the specific command at *sudo*. You need to type ***"sudo !!"***. The two exclamation marks mean run the previous command.

Try it:

```
sudo !!
```

Write to the file:

```
test 343
```

Success!

What if you have a lot of things to do, and you don't want to write *sudo* before every single command? You could do this using the *"su"* command, which means *switch user*. Generally, you type switch user, or *"su"*, followed by the name of the user account that you want to switch use.

You can type *"sudo su"* and this will move you to the root account. The root user has *100%* control of everything.

Try it:

```
sudo su
```

And now that you are in the root, create a file:

```
nano file
```

Jerry Banfield & Nick Germaine

Write to the file:

```
This is a new line
```

Save and close the file.

When you want to switch back to your user account, type *"su username"*, using your user name.

If you get a permission error when running a command, you may need to run that command as *sudo*. For instance, if you're editing files in a directory other than your *home directory*, you won't have permission to edit those files. Later we will look at how to get permission to edit those files, but for right now, this is when you would run your command prepended by *sudo*.

If you have a lot of these commands to run, and you don't want to type *sudo* before every command, just type *"sudo su"*.

Using the Package Manager to Install New Applications

In this section you will learn how to use the package manager in *Ubuntu* and how to manage the packages that have been installed or that you may want to install. We will be using a program called *"aptget"*.

In *Terminal* if you type *"apt-get"*, it will run a program used to install applications. If you followed this with *"install"* and the name of the application, and then hit **Enter**, this action will cause *apt-get* to perform installation. Let's try to install a text editor called *Bluefish*.

Try it:

```
apt-get install bluefish
```

You may get a message telling you that you do not have permission to use that program. This is where *sudo* comes into play. Type *"sudo !!"* and hit **Enter**.

The *apt-get* command will install *Bluefish*, along with bluefish-data and bluefish-plugins, which are two different packages that *Bluefish* needs. You'll see some information about how much data will be downloaded and how much space will be used on the disc after the application is installed. You see a message: Do you want to continue?: Type *"y"* for *yes* and hit **Enter**. It will connect to the repositories of *Ubuntu*.

Ubuntu has repositories set up that have indexes and package files. This allows you to run the command *apt-get* and install packages from the repositories. There are some programs that are not in the repositories. We'll go over those later. For this example, I know that *Bluefish* is in the repositories, and I knew the name of the package that I wanted to install before I ran the command. I could type *"sudo apt-get install bluefish"* and this installs *Bluefish* to my computer.

When the installation completes, you can click the **Super key** and type *"bluefish"* in the search field, or you can type *"bluefish"* in *Terminal*. In both cases you will see that *Bluefish* has been installed. And that's how you install programs.

Let's say you want to remove a program. You do that in a very similar way.

Try it:

```
sudo apt-get remove bluefish
```

With this command, you use the program *apt-get*, use the action *"remove"*, and the action is performed on the package *"bluefish"*. When you see the question, type **"y"** to mean *yes*, I do want to uninstall this. The package will be uninstalled.

What if you want to install the program and you're not sure of its name? We'll look at how to do that in the next section.

Searching the Repository to Find New Applications to Download

Let's say you want to search the repository and you're looking for something specific. You would use an *asterisk*. The *asterisk* means it will find anything that has the word *"bluefish"* in it.

Use this command:

```
apt-cache search bluefish*
```

Try this one:

```
apt-cache search gimp*
```

It returns a lot of stuff, but not *Gimp*, which is an open-source photo editor. Let's say you want to see if you have something, such as *Gimp*, already installed.

Try it:

```
apt-cache policy gimp
```

If you have *Gimp* installed, you'll see it, along with the version. If the official repositories contain this version, it means you've already installed *Gimp* through the repositories. You can also go to *Gimp's* website and download an installer file from there. If you're on an older version of *Ubuntu* that doesn't have the current version of *Gimp* in the repositories, you can manually install that package file. We will go over that later.

Try:

```
apt-cache policy bluefish
```

You just uninstalled it, but you'll find that you can install a *version 2.2* from the official repositories.

Installing a Package Not in the Repositories

What if you want to install a package that is not in the repository?

Search for Chrome:

```
apt-cache search chrome*
```

You will see a lot of *Chrome*, but not a package called *Chrome*. You will see *chromium–browser*, which is the open source version of *Chrome*.

You could install it:

```
sudo apt-get install chromium-browser
```

But let's say you want the actual *Google Chrome*. It's not under *Chrome*, and it's not under *Google Chrome* either. *Terminal* wasn't able to access that package in the repositories.

Use *Firefox*, the browser preinstalled on *Ubuntu*, to search for a *Chrome* package online. You can install other web browsers. If you wanted to install *Midori*, another web browser, you could check for a version in the repositories, and there is one. But you don't want to use the Midori. You want *Google Chrome.*

In *Firefox*, go to *https://www.google.com/chrome/browser/ desktop/index.html* and download the *Chrome* package. You'll have four options for downloading *Chrome*: *a 32 bit .deb file, 64 bit .deb, 32 bit. rpm and 64 bit .rpm.* We don't use *.rpm* files on *Linux*. That is the package manager for *Red Hat*, which is a different *Linux* version altogether. With *Debian-Ubuntu* distributions, you will use *.deb* files. *Apt Package Manager* works with *.deb* files. **Download** the *64 bit .deb* file, because you are likely working on a *64-bit* system with a *64-bit* installation. **Accept**, and **save** the file.

Once the download completes you can change directory to */home/Downloads* to find it.

Try it:

```
cd ~/Downloads
```

Find the file by running a list of the contents of /
Downloads:

```
ls
```

How are you going to install it? You could open the file
manager, go to the **Downloads folder**, double-click, and this
would open it with *Software Center*, which is *Ubuntu's*
graphical package manager app. But because we are
focusing on command line, you will install this package by
running a command.

Install Chrome:

```
sudo dpkg -i ./google-chrome-
stable_current_amd64.deb
```

The *"-i"* stands for *install*. Then you'll give it the file path of
the installation you want it to find. This will unpack this *Debian*
package and install *Chrome*. In *Terminal*, you can now type
"google-chrome" and launch it.

Keeping Programs Updated in Ubuntu Linux

The package manager doesn't only allow you to install and remove programs; it also allows you to keep things updated.

Let's say that a new package version of one of your applications has been pushed to the repositories. You can type *"sudo apt-get upgrade"* and this will upgrade any packages that have new versions in the repositories.

A little note on sudo: When you run it once in a session of *Terminal*, you don't have to put your password in every time; just the first time.

Let's take a look at doing upgrades.

When you find a package that needs to be upgraded, type *"y"* for *yes*, and hit **Enter**. All existing packages with available upgrades will be upgraded.

We covered a lot, so let's review.

In the package manager of *Ubuntu* and *Debian* and all *Debbian*-based distributions is *Aptitude*, which you get through a program called **apt-get**. You use *apt-get* to carry out specific actions, like installing programs and removing them. You can also add repositories, even repositories that are not in the official *Ubuntu* repositories, which will give you access to more applications.

You can use the ***"apt-cache"*** program to search through available applications and check the installed versions against new versions in the repositories. You can see programs that you already have installed by using the policy action in the *apt-cache* program.

You can use the ***dpkg*** application to install *.deb* files. This allows you to install packages that are not in the official *Ubuntu* repositories or other repositories.

You can manually download files, making sure the architecture is based on your hardware. In other words, if you're on a *64-bit* system, make sure that you are installing *64-bit* applications.

And the final piece is upgrading software. Periodically different package maintainers or developers will release new versions of their software into the repositories, whether that is the official *Ubuntu* repository or a third party repository that they manage and that you have added to your system. Using the ***"sudo apt-get upgrade"*** command allows you to upgrade packages that are available for upgrade.

File Permissions and Ownership

In this section you will learn more command line and how it's used for file permissions and file ownership.

You will need a file for which you don't currently have write permissions. The easiest way to create this file is to add a file as administrator using *nano*.

Create a new file:

```
sudo nano file.txt
```

Add example content to the file:

```
Read
```

Save and Exit:

```
CTRL O; CTRL X
```

Now if you type *"ls -l"*, you will see that *file.text* is owned by the *root* user and the user group is called root. You'll also see permissions. They tell you that the *owner* can read and write, that groups can only read, and that public can only read.

They look like this:

Owner: **-rw**

Group: **r--**

Public: **r--**

If you want to give yourself permissions to read and write, you need to change the third column, **r--**, to match the first column, **-rw**.

But first you need to share it with your user *group* by using a command to change ownership and replace *user* and *group*. Then, add the name of the file on which you want to perform the action. The command looks like this:

```
sudo chown user:group
```

Let's change the user to *root*, and the group to *nick*, or replace *group* with your *group* name.

Try it:

```
sudo chown root:nick
```

If you type *"ls -l"*, you should see that *file.txt* is now under the ownership of your *group*. Now, you need to change the third column for the public to *"write"* permissions.

You'll note that *6* means it is readable and writable, *4* means it is readable, and *7* means it's a directory. We don't use *7* with single files, but we'll go into that later. Let's say you want to change permissions from its current permissions, *644*, to *664*, which means the *owner* can read and write, the *group* can read and write, and the *public* can read only.

Change permissions:

```
sudo chmod 664 file.txt
```

Now if you type *"ls -l"*, you can see the change has been made. Now you can read and write to *file.text.*

Use *nano* for text editor:

```
nano file.txt
```

Write to it:

```
Write
```

Save and Exit.

Operations and Ownership

Well, that was neat. You gained access to a file to which you didn't have permissions. But let's say you want to own a file forever. Type *"sudo chown yourusername:yourusergroup"* and the name of the file you want to own. Say you want to switch the permissions back to *644*:

```
sudo chmod 644 file.txt.
```

Now you can delete that *file.txt*, because you don't need it. To delete a single file, use *"rm"* and then the filename.

Delete the file:

```
rm file.txt
```

List the directory:

```
ls
```

Note the file has been deleted.

Let's create a directory as an administrator. Use **"mkdir"**, which means to *make a directory*. You can name it *"mydir"*.

Create a new directory:

```
sudo mkdir mydir
```

You'll see the permissions after you run a list of the directory. It is owned by *user root* and *group root*.

Owner: **drwx**, meaning readable, writable and executable.

Anyone else: **-xr**, can read and execute it.

Change directory into *"mydir"*. This is called executing it. You've just allowed yourself to execute it, which allows you to go into the directory.

Go up one level in the directory:

```
cd ../
```

Create a new file and place it in *"mydir"*:

```
sudo nano ./mydir/file.txt
```

Now, if you *ls* that directory, you'll see the new file in *mydir*. If you type *"ls -l ./mydir"*, you'll see that file is owned by the *root*.

Let's make another file:

```
sudo nano ./mydir/file2txt
```

You can run the previous command in *Terminal* by using the *"up"* key. And if you keep hitting the *"up"* key, it will go up, up, up, to previous commands that you've entered.

Find two files in that directory that you want to own. It is likely *root* owns the files in the directory, because they were created using the super user account. You're going to change the form of ownership of a binary file by typing *"sudo chown"* and passing it in this argument, *"-R"*, which means it's recursive. Every file in this directory will be under your ownership.

Try it:

```
sudo chown -R user:group ./mydir
```

Let's look at this command in more detail, as it may be a bit confusing. You are running it as *sudo* because you don't have permissions to this directory; it's owned by the *root* user and group and you have no right to access it, so you can't change it.

The command *"chown"* stands for *change ownership*. That's the program you're running. You're passing it through the argument *"-R"* to make the command recursive. If you didn't use the recursive command, this would change the ownership of the directory to your username and your user *group*, but not the files in the directory.

Next, add the *user* and *group* that you want to receive ownership. And finally, add the file or directory on which you want to perform this action.

When you hit **Enter** and then type *"ls -l"*, you can now see that you have ownership of this directory. If you type *"ls -l"* on *"mydir"*, you can see that you also have ownership of everything within that directory.

Let's recap.

Change the ownership of the file: **chown**

Change the permissions of the file: **chmod**

Make it recursive: **-R**

Define the specifics of the changes you're making. So with the *"chmod"* command, you would use *755, 757* or *777*.

As a side note, if you're running a server, never make any directories ownership *777*. Files are one digit less than directories, so *666* would be full modification ability for anybody on the file. You never want to do that.

If you're using the *chown* command, it's going to be in the format *user:group*, and this will change the ownership of the file to which you are assigning it.

The last part of each of these two commands is the file or directory you want to affect. So, if you type */user/share*, this will give the user rights to all the files in this directory for this *user* and *group*. Be careful when you run that, because some files need to be owned by the *root* in order to work. Typically you will not be working much outside of your home directory, but we will get there. There are some files you will need to change, especially when you set up *Apache* as the web server.

Create a New File in the Terminal

Let's create some new files in *Terminal*. Change directory to */mydir* just because it can be quicker to write commands. If you want to create a file without opening it, type **nano** and then the *name of the file*.

If you just want to stay in *Terminal* and don't want to go into a text editor, you just want to create files, you can use **"touch"** followed by the filename: *touch file1.txt file2.txt file3.cpp file4.cpp*

Let's create a file called *"main.cpp"*:

```
touch main.cpp
```

Earlier, you learned how to use the *asterisk*. If you remove *.cpp* files, an *asterisk* would remove everything that has a *.cpp* extension: ***rm ./*.cpp***

If you want to remove everything but leave the directory intact, you would not include the .cpp files: ***rm ./****

Let's get out of this directory and see how it looks from the outside.

Go to the root:

```
cd ../
```

List the root directory:

```
ls
```

To remove everything in */mydir* without removing the directory:

```
rm mydir/*
```

If you run then run ***ls*** on */mydir*, you'll see it is empty. To remove */mydir*, you need to add the ***"-rf"*** command: ***rm -rf***

mydir

And now you're back where you started.

Let's recap a few commands. The command *"cp"* is copy. The first argument is the file and the second argument is where you want to place it and what file name you will use.

Copy a file:

```
cp file ./mydir/file2
```

Remove files:

```
rm file.txt
```

Remove file from another directory:

```
rm dir/file.txt
```

Remove all files with a certain extension:

```
rm dir/*.txt
```

Remove everything from a directory:

```
rm dir/*
```

Remove the directory and everything in it:

```
rm -rf mydir/
```

Create a file and stay in Terminal:

```
touch
```

If you want to move a file, rather than copying it, use the *"mv"* command, followed by the filename and the new filename. For example, move a file in the same directory with a new name: *mv filename filename2*

Spend some time copying and moving files around in *Terminal*. Be careful about changing permissions. For now, work in your *home directory*.

Creating New Directories and Moving Files

Let's cover a few more utility commands and then move on

to more advanced material.

We've been looking at utility commands that help you move around the file system, modify files and change permissions. We have a few more commands to learn.

Let's start by listing directory contents. Take a look at the *a.out* file. Let's say you want to move it. First, create a new directory.

The first command you'll use is *"mkdir"*, which is an abbreviation for *"make directory."* You'll follow it with the name of the directory that you want to create, and you can use an absolute position. You can go up one or two levels and create the directory, or just create it in the current place by typing the name. We'll call it *"newDirectory"*. Let's create the new folder in the current directory:

```
mkdir ./newDirectory
```

When you run *ls* again, you can see the new directory. Now, try moving *a.out* into */newDirectory*:

```
mv a.out newDirectory/a.out
```

This will take the file, which is in the current directory, and move it to /newDirectory. If you run ls on /newDirectory, you can find the *a.out* file there. It is no longer in the */home* directory.

Previously, you created a directory called */mydir*. Here's how you would rename */mydir*:

```
mv mydir mySecondDirectory
```

Now, let's copy the *a.out* file to the renamed directory. You'll do this by using the **"cp"** command for copy, followed by the file you want to move, followed by where you want to move it:

```
cp newDirectory/a.out
mySecondDirectory/a.out
```

If you list directory for */mySecondDirectory* and for / *newDirectory*, you'll see two copies of the *a.out* file.

Copying, Renaming and Removing Files

Let's say you want to copy a file and rename it. Just run

the copy command, name the file you want to copy, and then give it a new name:

```
cp ./newDirectory/a.out ./
newDirectory/b.out
```

List /newDirectory, and you'll see the a.out and b.out files.

Now, you have three copies of the same file. Let's move it back to the /home directory. Start from your /home directory. Change directories if you are not currently in your /home directory, and move a.out back to the /home directory, which is now your current directory:

```
cp ./newDirectory/a.out ./a.out
```

The a.out file is back where it started.

Now, remove the b.out file from /newDirectory. Don't forget to change directories:

```
rm b.out
```

It's that easy. The **rm** command removes the file. If you run **ls**, you'll see the *b.out* file has indeed been removed.

Go back up a directory:

```
cd ../
```

Earlier you created an entirely new directory. Let's remove it:

```
rm -rf newDirectory
```

Now, rename */mySecondDirectory* back to */mydir*, which will take it back to the name it had when you originally created it:

```
mv mySecondDirectory mydir
```

List */mydir* and you'll find three files that you've created: *a.out, file2.txt,* and *file.txt*. Let's remove all of the *.txt* files:

```
rm mydir/*.txt
```

If you had many files named the same, for example, *main.txt*, *main.cpp*, and *main.out*, you could remove all of the files named main:

```
rm mydir/main*
```

Remember, the *asterisk* just means *"everything"*.

CHAPTER 6

Moving on to More Advanced Commands in the Terminal

```
total 980K
drwxr-xr-x 24 aled aled 4.0K Jul 28 23:34 solarized
-rw-r--r--  1 aled aled 970K Jul 29 20:12 solarized.tar
aled@rose:~/archives$ du -mhs solarized
1.5M    solarized
aled@rose:~/archives$ tar -cjf solarized.tar.bz2 solarized
aled@rose:~/archives$ ls -lh
total 1.2M
drwxr-xr-x 24 aled aled 4.0K Jul 28 23:34 solarized
-rw-r--r--  1 aled aled 970K Jul 29 20:12 solarized.tar
-rw-r--r--  1 aled aled 160K Jul 29 20:13 solarized.tar.bz2
aled@rose:~/archives$ tar -czf solarized.tar.gz solarized
aled@rose:~/archives$ ls -lh
total 1.3M
drwxr-xr-x 24 aled aled 4.0K Jul 28 23:34 solarized
-rw-r--r--  1 aled aled 970K Jul 29 20:12 solarized.tar
-rw-r--r--  1 aled aled 160K Jul 29 20:13 solarized.tar.bz2
-rw-r--r--  1 aled aled 172K Jul 29 20:14 solarized.tar.gz
aled@rose:~/archives$ tar -cf solarized.tar.lzma solarized --lzma
aled@rose:~/archives$ ls -lh
total 1.5M
drwxr-xr-x 24 aled aled 4.0K Jul 28 23:34 solarized
-rw-r--r--  1 aled aled 970K Jul 29 20:12 solarized.tar
-rw-r--r--  1 aled aled 160K Jul 29 20:13 solarized.tar.bz2
-rw-r--r--  1 aled aled 172K Jul 29 20:14 solarized.tar.gz
-rw-r--r--  1 aled aled 138K Jul 29 20:15 solarized.tar.lzma
aled@rose:~/archives$
```

Getting Started with the Find Command

In this chapter, we'll get started by learning about the *"find"* command and it's practical uses. To get started, create a new directory called *"It"*, and change to that directory.

Then, create several files in that directory: *touch file.php file2.php file3.php another.php somethingelse.PHP anewone.PHP one.PHP two.txt three.txt four.TXT an.TXT*

While this is not a large directory, this will illustrate how you can use the find command. Note that some of the files are *.php* and some are *.txt*. Some are in all caps and others are not.

To use find, you'll use the following commands: **find**; *"."* to search the current directory; **-type**, which is a flag; **"f"** for *"file"*; **-name**, which is a flag for the name of the file you are searching; **"-iname"** to ignore cases sensitivity; and *"*"* for everything.

Find all files with the .php extension:

```
find . -type f -name "*.php"
```

You'll note that only files with the lowercase *.php* extension are returned.

Now, find all files with the *.php* extension, regardless of case:

```
find . -type f -iname "*.php
```

In this case, all files are returned with the *.php* extension, regardless of case. This command would even find files with a mixed combination of the extension, for example *pHp*.

The Find Command

You can also use the find command to find file names, not just extensions:

```
find . -type f -iname "file*"
```

There are other practical applications for the find command. You can search, for example, all configuration files in a named directory:

```
find /etc -type f -iname "*.conf"
```

You'll note this is a recursive function. It finds all files, even those in subdirectories.

The *-type* flag can be used in several ways: **"-type f"** will find only files; **"-type d"** will find only directories; omitting **"-type"** will find both files and directories.

To find files with certain permissions, use the *"-perm"* command for permissions, and then enter the numerical equivalent of the permissions you want to find. Remember, in a previous chapter you learned about these numerical equivalents:

```
find . -type f -perm 0664
```

You can also search based on file size. For the size of the file, you can enter an exact size or a *"+"* or *"-"* to indicate greater or less than:

```
find . -size +1M
```

You can also use a *"not"* operator. For example, you could find all files other than *.php*:

```
find  -type f  -not -iname "*.php"
```

The *etc* directory usually holds configuration files for applications. Earlier you used the find command to find all configuration files in the *etc* directory and noticed that it was recursive. But what if you don't want it to be recursive? You can control the level of the depth you want to find. For example, look for configuration files at one level:

```
find . -maxdepth 1 -type f -iname
"*.conf"
```

You can also use **"-maxdepth"** to find file of a certain size. Find files over *55k*:

```
find . -maxdepth 2 -type f -iname
"*conf" -size +55k
```

Introduction to the GREP Command

In the last section we looked at how to find files. The *GREP* command finds things in files.

Let's say you've created some *.php* files with functions that you've written to those files. Let's look for them in a file called *"another.php"*:

```
nano another.php
```

They may look like this:

```
function makeSandwich($bread, $meat,
$cheese){} and function
eatSandwich($sandwich){}
```

Use the *"grep"* command to search for those functions within a particular *.php* file. Follow the *grep* command with the type of file you want to find, and then where you want to search:

```
grep "function" another.php
```

You can even search in multiple files:

```
grep "function" file1.txt file2.txt
```

The grep command can take two flags:

The *"-i"* means ignore the case:

```
grep -i "function" ./*
```

The **"-n"** means line number where the instance is found:

```
grep -n "function" ./*
```

GREP

How do you use find with *grep*?

First, you enter a typical find command:

```
find . -type f -iname "*.php"
```

Then you execute using the **"-exec"** flag. The *-exec* flag must be closed with curly brackets and the plus sign. The full command line would look like this:

```
find . -type f -iname "*.php" -exec grep -i -n "function" {}+
```

The previous command will search all *.php* files and find case insensitive function files, including the line numbers.

You can group search parameters using find and grep:

```
find . -type f -size -55k -iname
"*php" grep -i -n "function" {}+
```

You can see that you can use *find* and *grep* together to search specific file types for a very specific string of files.

How to Redirect the Output of a Command

Rather than outputting the results of a command, you can redirect the results and place them into a file using this command:

```
ls > outfile.txt
```

You can then view the output of that command:

```
nano outfile.txt
```

You can also use the redirect output with *find* and *grep*. Do a search and redirect the output to a new file:

```
find . -type f -size -55k -iname
"*.php" -exec grep -i -n "sandwich" {}+
> f.txt
```

If you open *f.txt*, it will show you the two sandwich functions, but it won't print it out on the screen. So, you'll use *"| tee"* the command. This is useful if you want to copy the results of a command and see them in real time:

```
find . -type f -size -55k -iname
"*.php" -exec grep -i -n "function" {}+
| tee of.txt
```

Using the TOP Command to View Applications

In this section, we'll learn about processes, what they are, and how you can manage them.

If you've ever opened up the task manager in *Windows*, you would see a list of running applications, or processes. The same thing is true for *Linux*. A process is just an application that is running. You can get an idea of what kind of processes run on a *Linux* machine by using the command *"top"*. If you run *top*, it'll show the list of running applications. It's real time, so if you start new applications, it's going to show these process in the list.

Let's look at a few of the things you'll see in the list and what they mean. The *PID* is the process *ID* and you can use this to manage that process. The *USER* identifies who is running the application. You can see how long an application's been open, as well as the command that's associated with the process. And, as always, you can use *CTRL + C* to escape that.

How to view the entire list of processes and closing applications

To see the entire list, use a command called **"ps aux"**, which captures data at the time you run the command. It is not real time, but if you run the command, you can see the list is quite a bit larger. You can go through and look for applications that you want to see, but this can get a little convoluted because of how large this list can get.

Try running an application, such as a browser. I'll use the example of *Liri* browser. This is a process that is running. Now, you can run **"ps aux"** and pipe that over to the command *grep*, followed by the name of the process:

```
ps aux | grep liri-browser
```

This will search for all processes that have *Liri* browser anywhere. The name of command or the file path of the command doesn't matter. It will find the process based on that name. Now that's pretty neat. It returns a few things in the list. It gives you the process *ID*, the time running, the command, the time that it was run, etc. You could use this process *ID* to manage whether this app is running or not.

But let's say you have a few instances running. Open the browser in three more instances. Now you have three processes for the *Liri* browser running. What happens when you run the previous command? It's messy. You could read through this if you wish, but if you just want to have a quick look at it, this is not the command to use.

If you want to get the process *IDs* of an application you can use the ***"pgrep"*** command and type in ***"liri-browser"*** and this will return three process *IDs*, because you have three processes running:

```
pgrep liri-browser
```

The order of these process *IDs* is chronological, so the top one is the first browser window you opened, and so on. Let's say you wanted to close the second window. You can use a command called *"kill"*. You would type *"kill"*, then *"-9"* and then the process *ID*. In my example, the process *ID* for the second instance of the browser is *6300*. The command line would look like this:

```
kill -9 6300
```

If you run *pgrep* on *Liri* browser again, it will just show you the other two. You can kill apps in this way by adding all of the process *IDs*:

```
kill -9 6386 6358
```

But what if you don't want to type the process *IDs* for each one? You can close them all at once by using the *"killall"* command, followed by the process name:

```
killall liri-browser
```

What is a Service?

In the last section, we looked at processes. In this section, we'll talk discuss services, which are a special type of *Linux* process.

You'll want to download **Elasticsearch** from www.elastic.co. I've tried different versions of their software and find that version *1.7.3* works best on all *Debian* derivatives on which I've tried it. They offer *.deb* and *.rpm* installers.

We won't go into depth on *Elasticsearch*, but we will use it as an example of a service. We'll look at services more in-depth in a future chapter when we install *Apache* web server.

You can start a service by typing **"sudo service"** and then the service name, and then the action you want to perform, which is *"start"*:

```
sudo service elasticsearch start
```

You won't get an output, but the service does start. You can confirm this by going into *Firefox* and to the web interface of *Elasticsearch* at *http://localhost:9200/*

You will see that you are indeed connected to *elasticsearch*.

You can stop the service using a similar command:

```
sudo service elasticsearch stop
```

Then you can check the local host again and see that it is unable to connect, because it is no longer running the service.

A service is like a process, except you start it up, and it waits in the background until you need to use it, or it can perform various tasks in the background. Services are helpful to have, and they are lighter on the system when you are not using them.

Configuring Services Using the Command Line

Let's start up that service again and confirm that it's open.

Let's say you don't want to run it on port *9200*, but you

want to run it on port *1150*. You need to edit the configuration file. The *Elasticsearch* configuration file has the *.yml exten sion*. You can use find to look in the */ect* directory:

```
find /etc -type f -iname
"elasticsearch*
```

The command you want to use to edit the configuration file looks like this:

```
sudo nano /etc/elasticsearch/
elasticsearch.yml
```

You can then search for the part of the file that configures the port. You'll find it near the bottom. You'll see the *IP* address, then the port. The port default is *9200*. You can change it to *1150*, save the file, and exit.

If you refresh localhost, you'll notice that you are still running on port *9200*. It won't switch to port *1150* until the service is reloaded or restarted. For now, it is still using the old configuration file. Rather than typing the commands *"elasticsearch stop"* and *"elasticsearch start"*, you can use one command:

```
sudo service elasticsearch restart
```

Give it a moment to restart, and then refresh the system. You'll now be connected on port *1150*. The restart function has updated the configuration file, and it will no longer work on port *9200*.

That is basically how you run a service. We went through the commands that I learned when I was learning *Linux*, but we don't use those anymore. *Ubuntu.* has moved to using **upstart** and system control. So, let's stop a service. It's similar.

Let's use a different program:

```
sudo systemctl start elasticsearch
```

Essential system control does the exact same thing that the service command does; it just does it a bit differently, and that will probably become the standard way to do it in the future, so I recommend you know how to use it. The only difference between using service and system control is that in the system control the action comes before the program, or before the service name. With service, you type service, service name and then the action.

Using Crontabs and Cronjobs

Crontabs and *cronjobs* allow you to schedule tasks to be run at certain times. In *Terminal,* go to the interface for building crontabs:

```
crontab -e
```

This will open a *crontab* file. This will be saved in the */etc* directory. Erase the last line that shows you that the file is saved in the */etc* directory. This is so we can take a look at the previous line, which shows the structure of the crontab directory:

```
m h dom mon dow command
```

The structure of the *crontab* is as follows: minutes *0–59* minutes; hours *0–23*; day of the month *1–31*; month *1–12*; day of the week *0–6*; then the command that you want to perform.

Let's try it. Run the command on the *15th* minute *(substitute for a minute ahead of when you are running this command)*, the *14th* hour *(substitute for the hour when you are running this command)*, regardless of the day of the month, regardless of the month, regardless of the day of the week, and use the command *ls*. Output the command results to */home/user/lt/cronres.txt.*

The command will look like this:

```
15 14 * * * ls > /home/user/lt/
cronres.txt
```

Save and exit. Go to the directory in your user interface and look for *cronres.txt*. It should appear as soon as the time changes to the minutes and hour you indicated.

The process that you just ran should have returned a list of your home directory and placed it into the file you indicated. Why? Because of the exact time you indicated. On every day of the month, every month of the year, and everyday of the week, this action will be performed.

If you wanted to run this action at *5 a.m.* on *Sundays*:

```
00 05 ** 0 ls > /home/user/lt/
cronres.txt
```

The Practical Applications of Crontabs

That's cool, but what practical applications does it have? One of the applications, as you can see in the previous example, is that you can keep a backup updated. The backup will run at *5 a.m.* every week on *Sunday*, and it will create a var archive at */var/backups/home.tgz*. The contents will be the entire home directory. Basically, it will make an entire backup of all your files once a week. That's pretty useful.

Let's look at one more example of how crontabs can be used.

The reason I had you output your home directory for the *ls* command is because you created that *crontab* as a user, and so, if you wanted to run a command in a *crontab* that required elevated privileges, you would type *"sudo crontab -e"*. This would open the *crontab* file for the root user.

Let's set up a command. Let's run it at *7 a.m.* every day of the month, every month on *Monday*. Use the command *"apt-get upgrade -y"*. The *"-y"* flag in the *"apt-get upgrade"* command indicates *yes* to everything:

```
0 7 * * apt-get upgrade -y
```

This command will keep your system updated every week at *7 a.m.* on *Monday*. This is great for scheduling tasks if you need certain things to run at certain times or frequently.

I'm really excited about the next chapter. We're going to talk about developer issues. We will go over different development environments and technologies.

CHAPTER 7

Ubuntu Linux Developer Tools: Get Started as a Freelancer Today!

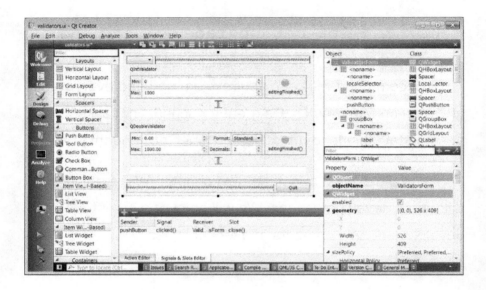

Choosing an integrated development environment (IDE)

In this chapter we will discuss integrated development environments, or *IDEs*, as they are called.

There's a difference between a code editor and an *IDE*. The code editor is good for quickly editing single files or multiple files, and they usually provide this syntax highlighting

Jerry Banfield & Nick Germaine

text, smart indentation, and sometimes code completion, which is a really handy to have.

However, if you are working on a large project or need a more complete set of tools for development, you will want to use an integrated development environment. *IDEs* offer the same code features as code editors, but also offer more advanced features like version control support, tool chains, and ways to run the application from right inside the *IDE*. Depending on your choice of programming language or development tools, you will need to choose an *IDE* that supports those technologies. Some *IDEs* support multiple languages, while others choose to support only one language or a select few. You will also need to optimize the *IDE* for the selected languages. For instance, *Eclipse* is a widely used *IDE* that provides version control support, as well as support for many different languages, including *C++, PHP* and *Java*.

Like many *IDEs*, *Eclipse* requires *Java* to be installed in order to use the *IDE*. To install the *Java* runtime in *Ubuntu*, open *Terminal* and run:

```
sudo apt-get install openjdk-8-jre
```

If this version is not available in your system repositories, you can install open *jdk7*. Then, extract the *Eclipse* archive you downloaded, and run the *"eclipse-inst"* file to launch a graphical installer.

Code Blocks is another popular *IDE* that supports *C++* and *Fortran*. Unlike *Eclipse*, *Code Blocks* was written in *C++* and some java script, therefore, it doesn't require any special runtimes in order to use it.

Qt is a framework for cross-platform *GUI* applications. The development installation includes its own *IDE* called *Qt Creator*, which supports *C++* and *QML* languages, version control, project and build management, and includes its own graphical *GUI* builder called *QT Designer*. *QT Creator* is the smartest *IDE* I've used. It can be very powerful when used correctly.

For everything other than *C++* and *QML*, I use *JetBrains IDE*. *JetBrains* is a company that provides *IDEs* for a variety of languages. No matter which of their *IDEs* you install, they will operate essentially the same way, but for different technology. They include great code completion and build management, as well as version control, a comprehensive settings component, and plugin support. When you write

Python code, it even lets you know if you violate any of the *PEP* guidelines, which is the style guide for *Python* code. It keeps things clean and readable.

Eclipse Installation and Setup

Once you download *Eclipse*, you'll get a compressed archive that you can right-click and extract. This will result in a directory called */eclipse-installer*. Double-click the installer and go into that directory. Once in that directory, right-click and then select **Open** in *Terminal*. You need to make sure that *Java* is installed.

I have had limited success with *jdk-8* using *Eclipse*, so install open *jdk-7*:

```
sudo apt-get install openjdk-7-ire
```

To confirm that you have *Java* already installed, type ***"java -version"***, and you should see what installation of *Java* you have.

To run the installer, target the current directory and run ***eclipse-inst***.

This will launch the *Eclipse* installer. Once the installer opens, you'll see a list of *IDEs* that you can install. If you download the complete package, it will show you every possible option. For now, let's just install the *Eclipse IDE* for *Java*. Click **Install**, and this will install *Eclipse* to your */home* directory. *Eclipse* directory will be set up, and then any *IDEs* that you install will be placed into that directory.

Next, the system will ask if you trust these certificates. Select all if you are confident this is the actual application. When the installation completes, you will be presented with a launch button. Go ahead and launch, and let's dive into *Eclipse*.

I don't use *Eclipse* for development, but if you do, and if this is something that you use on *Windows* or *OS X* and feel comfortable doing so, then you may want to use this on *Linux*. It's cross-platform, so everything should look the same.

Let's create a new *Java* project. In the *Eclipse IDE* interface, click **File/New/Java Project**. You can name the project *"untitled"*, unless you want to be more creative. Go ahead and click **Next** until you reach the **Finish** screen. You can leave all parameters on default for now.

When the project opens, you see a project explorer on the left, which is basically just a list of projects used in your *Eclipse* workspace, along with the *Java* project you just created. Now you can get started using *Eclipse*.

PyCharm Installation and Setup

Let's look at a *JetBrains IDE*. **Download** the *JetBrains IDE* and install it. The same goes for *PyCharm* or any *IDE* that you download. You will find a compressed archive file, and you'll need to extract it. As a result, you'll get a directory.

Go into the *IDEs* directory and into the */bin* directory. Right-click and **Open** in *Terminal*. This is *PyCharm*, so let's run the *pycharm.sh* file. If we were using *WebStorm*, there would be a file called *webstorm.sh*. This is pretty self-explanatory, so adapt to whatever *IDE* you have downloaded and are using.

To launch *PyCharm*, run the ***"sh"*** in the current directory:

```
sh ./pycharm.sh
```

The first time you launch *PyCharm* in this way, you will be prompted to create a *.desktop* file and *.mime* type associations. The *.desktop* file is basically a launcher in *Linux* and allows you to launch it through the dash overview or whatever you are using. If you have a menu from which you can launch apps, your apps will be created as entries in the menu.

Every time you launch *PyCharm*, you will see a list of projects on the left-hand side. Let's just create a new project. Click **Create New Project.** Select **Pure Python** and name it *"pi"* by changing the *"untitled"* in the **Location** field. It will scan all of the files in the project; right now there should not be many.

Again, on the left-hand side you'll see the project explorer. Now, you can right-click **on the directory,** and go to **New/ File/Python File** and create a new file within that directory. Call this new file *"main"*. In the editor that opens, you can change the directory that appears simply by typing in the new directory path. Then type: ***print ("hello world")***

If you were just using text editor for this, you would code it all in text editor. Then you would go and open up the command line, navigate to your main file and run it through

Jerry Banfield & Nick Germaine

the command line. The great thing about an *IDE* is you can actually run from the *IDE* itself.

An *IDE* is full featured, and most of what you need to do while developing can be done from within the *IDE*. There are more options for *IDEs* on *Linux*, so feel free to explore if you wish. In the next section, we will discuss *Git*, which will be mostly command line, but we will come back to *PyCharm*.

PyCharm Installation Problem Resolved

If you have a problem installing *PyCharm*, manually create the *.desktop* file for *PyCharm*. Right-click the **pycharm.sh** file and click **Open** in *Terminal*. Run:

```
sh ./pycharm.sh.
```

It will automatically load the last project on which you were working, and that's not what you want right now, so cancel the project. On the *PyCharm* welcome screen, you will see a **Configure link** at the bottom. Click that link, and select **Create Desktop Entry**. If you get an error message that says, *"unable to locate suitable startup script"*, attempt to make it executable. You would right-click on the ***pycharm.sh*** file, go to **Properties/Permissions**, and check the box that says, *"Allow executing file as program"*. That works! You can also do this with the *ch mod* command.

Introduction to GitHub, Installation, and Setting up a Repository

In this section we will discuss *GitHub* and why you should be using version control for your projects.

Git is a great tool if you work in a team, on large projects, or if you're working on open source projects. *Git* allows multiple people to work on the same files, or on the same project, at the same time. It's pretty smart and allows you to control things such as merging conflicts. A merge conflict happens when the same block of code is edited or modified by more than one person. *Git* allows you to sort out conflicts. We will look at how to do that.

First, you need to install *Git*. Go to *Terminal* and type *"sudo apt-get install git git-extras"*. You must add *git-extras* as well as *git* because it gives you a little more control. We will go over some of the things in the *git-extras* package in terms of what certain commands do in *Git*.

Once the installation of *Git* is complete, go into the **PyCharm directory** for the project you just created:

```
ch PycharmProjects
```

We named it *pi*, so let's change directory to */pi*, and you'll see your files there. Now, let's initialize a *Git* repository in this location: *git init*

At this point you will have an empty repository. It has no information, and it doesn't know where it should sync. Next, go to https://github.com. You will create a repository for this project there.

If you don't have an account on *GitHub*, create one now. If you already have an account, sign in. Click the **plus sign** at the top, and then click **New repository**. Give it a name. It's a good idea to give it the same name as your project. In this case we will name it *"Python-pi-example"*. Initialize the repository with the *README* file. We can automatically pull. You'll see the repository and the *URL* for the repository. Copy the *URL* and go back to *Terminal*.

Run:

```
git remote add origin URL (for the
URL, paste what you just copied from
the GitHub page)
```

This is how to tell your local repository where to find its remote origin. And that's the repository that you see in the background in *Chrome*.

Hit **Enter**. If you don't get a confirmation, that means everything worked as expected. If you get an error, just try to follow the error message as close as you can. The *Git URL* that you will add as the origin always ends in *.git*, so pay attention to that as well.

How to Pull and Push Information From Your Repository

Now that you have *Git* installed and your *Git repository* set, you also need to configure your user account. You will do that using the *git config* command:

```
git config --global user.name "type
your username here"
```

Next, set up your email, using your full email address at the end of this string:

```
git config --global user.email
youremail@gmail.com
```

Now that the user is set up, you can pull from this repository and push to it.

Let's do a pull by running this command:

```
git pull
```

It will give you an error because it does not know exactly which branch is the upstream, or which branch from which you should pull or push. You have two options. You can either run **"git pull origin"**, and then the branch name, or you can set the upstream branch.

Let's set the upstream branch:

```
git branch --set-upstream-to=origin/
branchname (substitute the branchname
for the branch you need; it will
probably be "master")
```

Now, let's do a manual pull:

```
git pull origin branchname
```

If you run *ls* you can see the *README* file.

You can now run the upstream again. You'll see that you need to do a pull first. That tells your machine what repository for *"branch"* it should use, and then you can set the upstream to one of those branches. The repository on your local machine has to be aware of the branches first.

Now, you have a repository setup. Let's look at editing a file. Go to **PyCharm** and open the project we created earlier. You'll see the *README* file. Open it and write a quick description. Click **CTRL S** to save the file.

Let's push this change to the server. First, you need to add all of the files to the tracker, and secondly, you need to commit changes, and then you need to push. Go back to *Terminal*.

To add the file, you can run *"git add"* and the file name, or if you want to add all the changed files, you can run *"git add - A"*. Run the second option to add all of the files

Now you need to commit the files. You can commit files with the command *"git commit -m"* and then add the commit message, which is basically a headline for the changes you made. It should describe the changes you made and be less then *140* characters, because all of the description will not display if it gets too long. Let's name this one *"updated read me added main.py"* The command line will look like this:

```
git commit -m "updated readme, added main.py"
```

Let's push it. You could run *"git push branchname"*. Remember, if you haven't yet set the upstream, you would need to do that, but since you already set the upstream, you could just type *"git push"* and enter the *username* and *password*.

You'll see this command has been successfully pushed to the remote repository. If you go back and refresh the repository in *github.com*, you will see changed *README* file and that the *main.py* file has been added. You also have a new directory, which is for the *PyCharm IDE* and provides information to *PyCharm*, such as which files are currently open. If you close *PyCharm* and reopen it, *PyCharm* knows which files to open from your last session.

How to Remove or Ignore directories in Your Repository

Let's take a look at removing directories in the repository. Let's remove the *.idea* directory. You won't use the typical *"rm"* command as you would expect. Instead you run ***"git rm - r"*** and then the name of the directory. This won't remove all of the files. If you change directory, you'll note it's no longer there, and if you go to *PyCharm*, you will probably be notified that something has changed.

Let's run:

```
git commit -m "Remove .idea
directory"
```

Jerry Banfield & Nick Germaine

Then push using *git push*. Now, if you go back and refresh, the */.idea* directory is still there. So, let's try to remove it again.

Close **PyCharm**, and let's run remove again and remove it with *"-f"* because it has been modified:

```
git rm -r -f .idea
```

Then let's run *git push* again. If you refresh *GitHub*, you should see the directory is gone.

How do you ask *Git* to completely ignore that directory? It will be automatically created every time you launch *PyCharm* or whatever *JetBrains IDE* you are using. And, as we just saw, it creates a hidden directory that you don't necessarily want to be included in the repository. I believe it does this for most *IDEs*.

Get the name of the directory you want to ignore. In the main repository directory run:

```
git -ignore .idea/*
```

Now you should be able to see that the ignored directory has been excluded.

Open *PyCharm* and make some changes to the *main.py* file, and then commit those changes to the repository.

Open *main.py* and defined the main function text message:

```
def main(msg)
```

Let's print the message:

```
print(msg)
```

And call it main:

```
main ("Hello People")
```

And save it.

Now run this in the *IDE*. You want to make sure it works before you commit. Go to the menu and click **Run/Run** and the file you want to run. In the *Run* field in the lower portion of the screen, you should see **Hello People**, followed by

"Process finished".

Go back to Terminal and commit.

Run:

```
git add -A
```

Run:

```
git commit -m "changed main.py"
```

Run:

```
git push
```

Refresh, and you should see the *main.py* file is the newest version. The */.idea* directory is no longer there because we've ignored it. And that's how you use *Git* in *Terminal*.

How to Resolve Conflicts from the Command Line

Let's create a *merge conflict*. To set this up, create a new directory and using the instructions in the last section, add the same project to this new directory. You will then have two copies of the same directory. Now go in and make some changes to the file in the new directory. Now you have a file that is behind the master branch.

Typically, each day you would run *git pull* and *commit*, and probably throughout the day as others are working in the files. But if you forget to do that, you'll have a *merge conflict*.

Let's assume you continue working and you edit the file in the main */pi* directory. Go back into *Terminal* and change to the */pi* directory, if you aren't already there. Try to push your changes to the server and commit, without being aware that your local repository is behind the remote repository. You'll get an error message.

Run:

```
it fetch origin branchname
```

This will merge your changes with the changes on the server. You'll open the file on your local and see that the file now contains your comments and the comments that were committed to the server. You'll see some special characters that indicate the merged comments. You'll also see a note telling you which comments came from the remote server. For now, just delete those special characters and save both comments. Save the file.

Now you can go back into *Terminal* and add the file:

```
git add -A
```

Commit the file:

```
git commit -m "merged conflicts resolved"
```

Push:

```
git push
```

The conflicts are now resolved. Go back to the *Git* repository and refresh.

Merging conflicts is a useful skill to have.

How to Set Up and Manage Branches

If you have multiple people working on multiple features, you may want to create more than one branch. You can then merge branches back into the master. Let's set up a new branch.

Go into *PyCharm* and open the project in which you've been working. In the lower right-hand corner, click the drop down menu next to the current branch, and select **New Branch**. Enter the name of the new branch. Let's call this one *"v1"*.

Make some changes to the *main.py* file and save it. Then, push and commit the changes.

Run:

```
git add -A
```

Run:

```
git commit -m "new branch"
```

Run:

```
git push origin v1
```

If you go back to the repository, you'll see two branches. Use the drop down menu to see all branches and switch between them.

You can also merge branches back into the master branch. In this case, let's merge *branch v1* back into the *master branch*.

First, you need to go into *Terminal* and check out the *master branch*:

```
git checkout master
```

Merge v1 with master:

```
git merge v1 master
```

Push the master:

```
git push origin master
```

When you refresh, you'll see a *new commit* on the *master branch*.

Making Comments in Python

I should make one final comment about using *Python*. In *Python*, when you want to make comments in an actual file, use the *hashtag*. For example, if you open *main.py* and make some changes, you can add a comment preceded by the *hashtag*:

```
Def main(msg)

# This a comment about the change you made to the file

print(msg)

main("Hello People")
```

Getting Started with Meteor: Installation and Adding Packages

In this section we will look at *Meteor*, what it is, and how to use it.

First, in *Google*, type in the address bar type *"Install Meteor"*. This will give you the location of the *Meteor* installer to download.

Because you are working in *Linux*, you'll want to copy the *install URL* from that page. It's in a gray box and starts with *"curl"*. After you copy this link, open *Terminal*, and paste it here. If you get an error it means you don't have *Curl* installed and you need to install it.

To install *Curl*, type *"sudo apt-get install curl"*. Once *Curl* is set up, you can run the previous command again to download *Meteor* and install it. Once *Meteor* has been installed, you will receive a notice about how to get started.

Let's use *Meteor* to create an app. Change directory to / *projects* and type *"Meteor create todo"*. This will create a project and the project directory in my current directory called *"/todo"*.

Change directory to **/todo**, the directory *Meteor* created. You'll see three files to get you started. Type **"Meteor"** in *Terminal*, and the program will launch on port *3000*. You'll see a message that the app has been launched. You can go to *http://localhost:3000* and see the *Meteor* app.

When it opens, you'll see a simple app, an event handler for the click me button, which counts the number of times it's been pressed.

We are going to make some changes. To add packages to *Meteor*, type **"meteor add"** and the package name. Let's go search for a package.

You can browse *Meteor* packages by going to *www.atmospherejs.com.* Search for *Bootstrap* and you'll see quite a few options. Find the official *Bootstrap* module or package, and in *Terminal* add *Twitter Bootstrap*:

```
add twbs:bootstrap
```

You've added *Twitter Bootstrap* to your project.

Go into the file manager, into */Projects/todo* and you will see that three files were created. If you use *CTRL H*, you'll also see a hidden directory entitled *Meteor*. This is where the packages you added are stored, along with some internal media files. You'll be working in the files in /todo. You'll see *.css, .html,* and *.js*. For example, you can open the *HTML* file with a text editor and see the markup.

Meteor often uses templates. Let's look at how to get started. *Meteor* has a pretty awesome tutorial on their website at *www.meteor.com*. You can also access the documentation, reference points, and a tutorial to get you started.

For now, let's look at how to use *Meteor* in the command line. Typically, just type **"meteor create"** and the app name. Once you are in the app directory, run *Meteor* to run the application. You can use *"meteor add"* or *"meteor remove"* to add or remove packages. Just add the package name after either command.

One selling point is the fact that real-time interactions are built into *Meteor's* core, so you no longer have to fake it with *JavaScript, Ajax* calls and *PHP* scripts. Everything is done in *JavaScript,* and it's all real-time. If you are into web application development, you'll find that *Meteor* makes things easy.

Meteor Tutorial Part 1: Setting Up Your First Project

This section is for developers, and I think you will find it really helpful. We will take a more in-depth look at *Meteor* and how to use it in your project. We will discuss how to use *Meteor* with *React* and *Slow Router.* There's not too much information out there on this combination of tools, so it makes sense to give you this information. Perhaps you'll decide to use *Meteor* in your next project.

In the last section, you created a project through *Terminal* for *Meteor*. Open **Terminal** and change directory to ***/projects/ todo.*** As you saw, *Meteor* automatically created a few files for you. Go ahead and open this up in *WebStorm*. Click **Open** and go to ***Projects/todo***. *WebStorm* will open the project. You will see the project you created on the left-hand side. First, delete these files, because we don't need them: *todo.css, todo.html, todo.js*

You can create some new directories. Because projects can get fairly large in *Meteor*, you will be working with many files, therefore, organization is a huge benefit.

Right-click and create three directories: ***/client, /lib,*** and one more called ***/server.*** The */client* directory will contain everything that will be available to the client. This is where you will place templates and some other things. In the */client* directory, create a new directory called */components.* This is where you will store the *Reactor* components.

Go to the **/lib** directory and create a file called ***router.jsx***. In the router file, you will be defining routes for *FlowRouter*.

But before we get to that, you need to add some packages to the project.

Using *Terminal*, run:

```
meteor add react kadira:react-layout
kadira:flow-router
```

Hit **Enter**, and you've added everything you need for your packages.

Because I was having an issue with *JetBrains IDEs* and it was a conflicting with *open jdk*, I installed *Oracle Java* to resolve those issues. I found that when you start typing something, this auto-suggestion box pops up, and it was causing the program to hang. To resolve these issues, I had to add a repository to my system.

You can go to _www.launchpad.net_, find _Oracle Java JDK_, and copy the archive _URL_. Then, in _Terminal_, run:

```
sudo add-apt- repository
ppa:webupd8team/java && sudo apt-get
update && sudo apt-get install oracle-
java8-installer
```

You can start connecting multiple commands together. The _"&"_ tells _Terminal_ to run one command and when that's done, and if it is successful, run the second command, and then the next, and so on.

Run this installer and this should resolve the issues with jet brain _IDEs_.

Let's start making some routes.

Meteor Part 2: Setting Up Your Router and React Components

First, you need to set up the router to route to certain files and roots. Create the first route. In _Meteor_, go into the **_router.jsx_** file. Here's what you'll add to this file:

```
FlowRouter.route("/". {

name: "home",

action(params) {

renderView(<Home />)

}

function renderview(component {

ReactLayout.rende(MainLayout, {

header: <Header />,

content: component,

footer: <Footer />

logThis: "This is a property"

});
```

Let's create the main layout. We are telling it to render a **React** component, **MainLayout**, and pass it through the parameters that follow.

Go to **Client/Components** and create a new *React* class called *"MainLayout.jsx"*. This is how you create *React* components. Name the component and state what it is equal to. Add a *render function*. Then you can add *html*. You can access properties by using *console.log.* Here's how the *MainLayout.jsx* file will look:

```
MainLayout = React.createClass({

render(){

console.log(this.props.logThis);

return (

<div>

Test

</div>

)

}

});
```

Save this file, and go back to the app at *localhost:3000*.
Refresh. You'll see that *Home* is not defined because you
haven't created the component yet. Let's create the header.
Create a new file in *Components* called ***Header.jsx***. It will
look like this:

```
Header = React.createClass({

render(){

return (

<div>

<div className="navbar navbar-
default">

<div className="container">

<a className=navbar-brand>My Site
Name</a>

</div>

</div>
```

```
</div>

  )

  }

});
```

Let's create the footer. **Create** a new file in *Components* called *Footer*.

```
Footer = React.createClass({

render(){

return (

<div>

</div>

  )

  }

});
```

Then, create the *Home* component. To keep things organized, create a new directory in *Components* called **Home.jsx**:

```
Home = React.createClass({

render(){

return (

<h1>

Hello world

</h1>

)

}

});
```

Now when you refresh the page, you'll see it start to take shape, because you've rendered all of the references you made. Basically, you are passing components into the *MainLayout* component. So, you would reference header, content and footer in the very same way. Except, if you want to render the content of a property, you put it in single curly brackets. So it's like *Blaze*, except you're not using two curly brackets; you're just using one.

Back in the *MainLayout.jsx* file, add these lines between **<div></div>**:

```
<div>

{this.props.header}

{this.props.content}

{this.props.footer}

</div>
```

Refresh your page again, and you should see the basic components of your page layout. Make sure *Bootstrap* is still running. If not, go into *Terminal*, run *Bootstrap* and run *Meteor* again. Your page will refresh automatically, because it is *Meteor*!

Meteor Tutorial Part 3: Programming

Now, we're going to get into programming. In the *Server* **create** a new directory called ***Collections***. In this new directory, **create** a new file called ***Posts***. Here's what you'll add to the *Posts* file:

```
Posts = new Mango.Collection("posts")

Posts.allow ({

insert: function(){

return true:

}.

update: function(){

return true:

}.

remove: function (){

return true:
```

```
}.

});
```

You need to create a way to put the posts in here. **Create** a new component in *Home* called ***InsertPosts.jsx***:

```
InsertPost = React.createClass({

render(){

return (

<div>

<text area placeholder="Type a post"
className="form-control" id="post-
body"></textarea>

<button className-"btn btn-info">Save
Post</button>

</div>

)
```

```
}

});
```

Now, let's render it in the *Home.jsx* component:

```
Home = React.createClass({

render(){

return (

<div>

<h1>

Hello world

</h1>

<InsertPost />

</div>

)

}

});
```

When you refresh the page, you'll see the new **Insert Post** component has been rendered. But when you type into the post area, it doesn't save. So, let's add and change some things to *InsertPosts.jsx* to get this page working. Once you start getting more functions in *React* components, you need to separate them with a comma. Here's what your *InsertPosts.jsx* file will look like with the additions:

```
InsertPost = React.createClass({

insertToCollection(event){

event.preventDefault();

var content = $("#post-body"). val();

Posts.insert({content: content,
dateAdded: new Date()});

},

render(){

return (

<div>
```

```
<form
onSubmit={this.insertToCollection}

<text area placeholder="Type a post"
className="form-control" id="post-
body"></textarea>

<button type="submit" className-"btn
btn-info">Save Post</button>

</div>

)

}

});
```

Now, if you go back and add content, it will be placed it into the database. But how can we get them out of the database and into the text area? Edit the **Home.jsx** component:

```
Home = React.createClass({

Mixins:[ReactMeteorData]
```

```
getMeteorData(){

var posts = Posts.find().fetch();

return {

posts: posts

}

render(){

let allPosts = this.data.posts;

return (

<div>

<h1>

Hello world

</h1>

<InsertPost />

</div>
```

```
)

}

});
```

And the **InsertPosts.jsx** file will look like this:

```
InsertPost = React.createClass({

insertToCollection(event){

event.preventDefault();

var content = $("#post-body"). val();

var user = $("#user").val();

Posts.insert({content: content, user:
user, dateAdded: new Date()});

},

render(){

return (
```

```
<div>

<form
onSubmit={this.insertToCollection}

<input className-"form-control"
id="user" placeholder="User Name" /
><br />

<text area placeholder="Type a post"
className="form-control" id="post-
body"></textarea><br />

<button type="submit" className-"btn
btn-info">Save Post</button>

</div>

)

}

});
```

Meteor Tutorial Part 4: Rendering Posts

To render your posts, in the home directory under components, **create** a new file called *Post.jsx*.

We're going to do something a little different, because each post that's rendered needs to be rendered as a single post. We are going to pass the post *ID* as a property to the function.

```
Post = React.createClass({

render(){

let {postID} = this.props;

return (

<div>

</div>

)

}
```

```
});
```

You can go in and test this by adding and saving some posts. Next, you'll add them to the page by adding some things to the **Home.jsx** file. The *Home.jsx* file will look like this now:

```
Home = React.createClass({

Mixins:[ReactMeteorData]

getMeteorData(){

var posts = Posts.find().fetch();

return {

posts: posts

}

},

getPosts(){

return Posts.find(). fetch();
```

```
},

renderPosts(){

return this.getPosts().map((post) =>
{

return <Post key={post._id}
post={post} />;

});

},

render(){

let allPosts = this.data.posts;

return (

<div>

<h1>

Hello world

</h1>
```

```
<InsertPost />

<br />

{this.renderPosts()}

</div>

)

}

});
```

And the **Posts.jsx** will look like this:

```
Post = React.createClass({

render(){

let {post} = this.props;

return (

<div className="card">

<h3>{post.user}</h3>
```

```
<p>(post.content)</p>

</div>

)

}

});
```

When you refresh, your posts should render on the page.

Meteor Tutorial Part 5: Putting on the Finishing Touches

You now have a new way to insert posts and view the posts. Let's say you have posts by two different people. *Meteor* should handle this in *React* and *FlowRouter*. Let's modify the **Home.jsx** component to use a different route.

Start with the **Router.jsx** file. Note that when you create new routes, you need to type **FlowRouter.route:**

```
FlowRouter.route("/". {

name: "home",
```

```
action(params){

renderView(<Home  />)

}

});

FlowRouter.route("/posts-by/:user", {

Name: "Posts",

action(params){

renderView(<Home user={params.user} /
>);

function renderview(component {

ReactLayout.rende(MainLayout, {

header: <Header />,

content: component,

footer: <Footer />

logThis: "This is a property"
```

```
});
```

And then the **Home.jsx** file should look like this:

```
Home = React.createClass({

Mixins:[ReactMeteorData]

getMeteorData(){

var posts = Posts.find().fetch();

return {

posts: posts

}

},

getPosts(){

if(this.props.user){

return Posts.find({"user":
this.propos.user}).fetch();
```

```
}else {

return Posts.find(). fetch();

},

renderPosts(){

return this.getPosts().map((post) =>
{

return <Post key={post._id}
post={post} />;

});

},

render(){

let allPosts = this.data.posts;

return (

<div>

<h1>
```

```
Hello world

</h1>

<InsertPost />

<br />

{this.renderPosts()}

</div>

)

}

});
```

When you refresh the page, you can view posts by user. In the *URL*, *localhost:3000/posts-by/username*, you can return the posts by each user who entered a post. But the *Home* page, *localhost:3000*, will return all posts.

That's an overview of *Meteor*. It works well with *React* and *FlowRouter*, and I highly recommend it.

Apache 2, PHP 5 and MySQL Installation

In this section we will focus on *Apache 2*, *PHP 5* and *MySQL*. In essence, you will configure and set up a lamp stack. This section is for beginners to install everything necessary and set up basic configuration. In the next section we will look at more advanced configurations.

Open *Terminal* and install all the necessary packages:

```
sudo apt-get install apache2 php5
mysql-server php5common
```

```
sudo apt-get install php5
```

```
sudo apt-get install mysql server
```

```
sudo apt-get install php5 common
```

Click **yes**, and it will download about *40 MB* of data, so this may take a bit of time depending on your connection.

Apache is the server that runs the *Internet* and basically allows you to host websites and such. If you were working with the server through *SSH* or something similar, you would be doing this to install *Apache* to serve web pages and content. That's why you would use *Apache*. Recently I found that I can't use *less.js* without going through the server and the domain. If you create a basic *HTML* file that uses *Less* and the *less.js* file, you can't just open *file://* and then the file path. You have to set up *Apache* and serve it as a web page on *localhost*.

MySQL is another *SQL* server more commonly used with *PHP*, and for good reason. It's good, it's just not my preference. I really like *Mongo DB*. *MySQL* is more compatible with *PHP*, from what I understand. You may use this if you are hosting a *WordPress* blog, or if you're using *PHP MySQL* development or maintaining something.

The *MySQL* service needs a *root password*. The username is *root* and the *password* will be whatever you choose. Then you'll need to retype it. That's the only user interaction required. It should return you to the prompt.

Getting Started With Your Server Configuration

Now that everything is installed and set up, you will start the *Apache2* service:

```
sudo systemcontrol start apache2
```

Then, you should be able to go to *http://localhost*, no port is needed, and you'll see the default *Apache2* web page.

Open file manager to see where *Apache2* serves the files by default. Go to ***Other Locations/Computer/var/www/html*** and **open** *index.html.* This index file is the same page you are seeing on *localhost.* You can open **Permissions** and see that *root* owns it. If you were to try to edit the file and save it, you wouldn't be able to do so. You must run everything in *sudo*, or *root*, and that's bad. We're not going to do that. We're going to make a few configuration changes.

Back in *Terminal*, run this recursively:

```
sudo chown -R username groupname /
var/www
```

If you go back into **Permissions**, you'll see the change.

The next change you need to make is within the configuration file of *Apache* itself.

Change to the */etc/apache2* directory and run *ls*. You're looking for the configuration file, so run:

```
sudo nano envars
```

Change the **APACHE_RUN_USER=** to your *user* and **APACHE_RUN_GROUP=** to your *group*. **Save** and **quit**, and then **restart** the server. If you were to refresh now and had made any major changes in configurations, they would not take effect until you restart.

Now you have the ability to edit this file. First, let's delete it and create a new file. **Delete** the *index.html* and go back into *Terminal*. Change directory to */var/www/html.*

Since you have write access, you no longer have to use *sudo*. Instead, run:

```
nano index.php
```

Then confirm that *PHP* is working:

```
?php

phpinfo();

?>
```

Refresh the **Apache2** web page. Now you can see the output of a configuration check for *PHP* and the server itself.

You can see how easy it is to set up *PHP* and *MySQL* in *Apache*. It's not really as complicated as you think to set up a server. You just install two packages, start the service, and you're good to go. I hope you were able to get your web server set up and running.

CHAPTER 8

What Is the Hosts File on a Linux System?

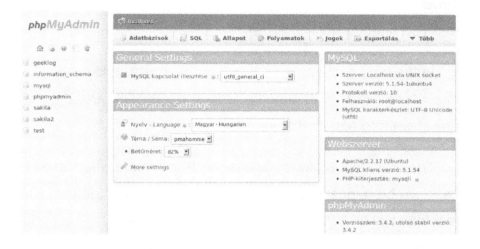

In this chapter we will touch briefly on the hosts file on a *Linux* system, what it is, and what it does, because we will be using it in the future. You will learn how to configure something in your hosts file

When you type in *google.com* in a browser, your computer first checks to see if there are any specified routes in your system to tell the system where *google.com* is located. If not, then it goes out to the Internet and takes a look. With the hosts file, you'll be intercepting requested domains from your machine.

Open *Terminal* and change directory to */etc*. Then type **"sudo nano hosts"**. There is a host file in the */etc* directory that you need to go in and get.

In the next section, we will be using a route called **"app.localhost"** to deploy the *Meteor* application. But right now, I want to explain how this works.

The first element in the line is the *IP address*, which in this case will be a local machine. The local *IP address* for any machine will be *127.0.0.1*. That will indicate that whatever you type in next should go to *localhost*, and then *Apache* will pick it up from there.

If you type in *google.com* and save it, when you try to go to *google.com*, it will take you to the *Apache* default page, which is the word at */var/www/html/index.html.*

You could configure a virtual host to handle *google.com* as its own virtual host, in order to serve up the specified web page from your local machine. We'll learn how to do that later.

For now remove *google.com*, because you don't want *Google* to always be redirected to your local machine. You can create a subdomain of *localhost* and call it *subdomains.localhost* and save it. Now if you go to *http:// subdomain.localhost,* you'll be redirected to the main *HTML* directory. You'll need this for the next few activities, as you will be redirecting certain *localhost* addresses and subdomains to your local machine. Then you'll get a patch to intercept them and serve content based on that.

Deploying the Meteor to an Apache 2 Server

Open *Terminal* and change directory into ***/Projects/todo.*** You will start to build *Meteor* app:

```
meteor build ../todo
```

This may take a while as it compiles the entire project into its final form. When complete, if you change directory up one level, you will find a */todo app* directory. Change to that directory. You need to copy the resulting *tar.gz* files to the *Apache HTML* directory:

```
cp todo.tar.gz /var/www/html
```

Go to the location where you placed it and extract it:

```
tar -xvf todo.tar.gz
```

When you run the *ls* command you should see a bundle directory. Go into that bundle directory and install ***node.js***. You won't be able to install from the repositories, as the version that's included in our repositories is different from the version you actually need, which is *0.10.29* or higher. So, you'll need to ask for a specific package, *www.ubuntuupdates.org/package/nodejs_v012/wily/main/ base/nodejs*

If you go to the *PPA* you'll see *Trusy*, *Utopian*, *Vivid* and *Wily*. We are on version *Wiley*, so it is grayed out. Choose the one that makes sense for your system and then click on the most recent package. Click **Download 64-bit deb package** to download it. It should open up in the **Software Center**. You'll be manually installing this.

Once it opens up, it will prompt you that an older version is included in your systems repositories, and it's recommended that you use that version instead, and only install this if you know what it is. You can disregard this message. This is the package we need. Click the **install button** on the right. Once

Jerry Banfield & Nick Germaine

it's finished, you can close the program.

Go back to *Terminal*, and from the bundle directory, run the **ls** command, and look at the structure of the directory. The **main.js** file will be of interest shortly; but for right now, change directory into **/programs/server** and run **"sudo npm install"**. This will reinstall *node.js* fibers. Now the app is ready to go, but we need to configure a few things. Change directory to **cd ../ ../**

Setting Up MongoDB NoSQL Database

You need to make sure *Mongo* is running:

```
sudo systemctl start mongodb
```

You can confirm it's running by going to *localhost:27017*. You'll get a message that tells you it's running.

You need to create a *user* for the database that the app will use. We will create a database called **"app"**. You need to connect it to the *Mongo* shell to create a user for it. To do this type **"mongo"** and it will take you in and automatically connect you to a test database. You need to be using your database, so enter the following command:

```
use app
```

Create a user:

```
db.createUser({name: "username", pwd
"password1", roles: [{role: "read
Write", db: "app"}]})
```

Make sure your syntax is correct. It's very easy to miss commas or brackets when working in the *Mongo* shell. Now you can just hit **Enter**, and it should create a user and tell you that it successfully created a user. Exit, and you'll be back in the shell.

Let's configure Mongo:

```
sudo nano /etc/mongodb.conf
```

You need to turn authentication on. Scroll down to **#autho = true**, remove the **#** symbol. Save and exit.

Restart Mongo:

```
systemctl restart mongodb
```

Now, you will configure *Apache*. This will be a more advanced configuration. You may need to use some different modules with *Apache* than what you needed with *Meteor*. If you are deploying a *Meteor* app, this should work flawlessly for you. But this gives you an idea that there are different modules that you can enable and disable in *Apache* if you need them.

You need to enable three modules for *Apache* to handle the proxy, because you'll be running your app on port *58080*, but you don't want users to have to remember the port number, and you definitely don't want the port number visible in the *URL*. So, this is what we will configure for *Apache*.

To start the configuration:

```
sudo a2enmod proxy
```

Run:

```
sudo a2enmod proxy_html
```

Run:

```
sudo a2enmod proxy_http
```

You need to create the virtual host. The virtual host would be used if you want to run, for example, six different websites in their own directories at six different domain names. Let's say you have one domain name pointing to this server, but you want to use subdomains, which is the portion for the domains. You can have *app.yourdomain.com* and *app2.yourdomain.com*. Here's how you would set those up:

Go into */etc/apache2*, where you can see that you have a */sites-available* directory. Create a file in there:

```
sudo./sites-available app.conf
```

Creating a Virtual Host

Now, you have a blank file, and you need to create a virtual host. First, open the element *VirtualHost*. Then specify the port where it is listening, which is port *80* by default for *Apache*. That's the default port for web traffic. The first thing you should do is assign the server name, which tells the virtual host to what name it should be listening.

Then, jump down a few lines and configure the proxy. You also need to configure the proxy for the correct ports. You'll also add a location element to tell the proxy to which host it should pass. Here's what your file should look like:

```
<VirtualHost *:80>

ServerName app.localhost

ProxyRequests Off

<Proxy *>

Order deny,allow

Allow from all
```

```
</Proxy>

<Location />

ProxyPass http://localhost:58080/

ProxyPassReverse http://localhost:
58080/

</Location>

</VirtualHost>
```

Save, and *Apache* is configured to translate *app.localhost* at port *58080* to the *URL* at *localhost*. Now you can exit.

Now that you've configured the virtual host, you can add to this site or enable it:

```
sudo a2ensite app
```

You have all of the modules enabled and the virtual host configured and enabled. You can restart the *Apache 2* service:

```
sudo systemctrl restart apache2
```

Using a Shell Script to Set Environment Variables

Change directory to the *HTML* directory:

```
cd /var/www/html/bundle
```

In order to run the *Meteor* application, you need to set a few environment variables. You can do this from *Terminal*:

```
export MYVAR="This is a variable"
```

If you are using digits or characters, you don't have to use quotes, but if you are using a string with spaces, you need to include the string in quotes.

Once you've created that variable, you would be able to echo that out in the shell by typing the same:

```
echo $MYVAR
```

There is a downside to creating variables in *Terminal*. As soon as you close *Terminal*, all of those environment variables will be lost. If you need to restart your app in a week, or you don't want have to retype all of the variables, you need to create a shell script that will do this for you:

```
nano ~/Documents//env.sh
```

The first thing you need is the *CrunchBang*, and you need to tell it the file type:

```
#!usr/bin/sh
```

This will tell it to run with *bash*; then you can just start creating your variables. You need three. The first one will configure the port to *58080*. That's the port on which the *Meteor* application will run. The next one is the root *URL* where the app will run. In this case it is *app.localhost*. Then you need to add a *Mongo URL*. This will be a *URL* using the *mongo.db* protocol, along with the *username*, *password*, *host name* and the *database "app"*.

Here's what it will look like:

```
#!usr/bin/sh

export PORT= 58080

export ROOT_URL=http://app.localhost

export MONGO_URL=mongodb://
username:password1@localhost:27017/app
```

Save and exit.

Let's say you need to restart the *app*, and you don't want to retype all of those variables and the values for them. You can rerun the script. Usually, to rerun the script, you would use the **sh** command and then the location of the script. But because the variables that we're exporting in that script need to be integrated into the environment where we are working, we will use the source command:

```
source ~/Documents/env.sh
```

Then echo the port:

```
echo$PORT
```

It will print out a report. Now you can run the application, and it should be good to go:

```
nodejs main.js
```

With no errors, you should be able to go to *http://localhost: 58080*. You should reach the *todo* app. You should also be able to go to *http://app.localhost*

This works, but as soon as you exit, you will see that the *app* is unavailable. When you exit out of a *nodejs* shell instance, it stops the *app*. In order to run this outside of this instance of *nodejs*, you need to install an *npm* application called *Forever.*

```
sudo npm install -g forever
```

The *-g* tells the command that you will globally install the following application. If you did not include *-g*, you would just install *Forever* to the current node instance, which is the

Meteor application. You wouldn't be able to use it elsewhere, unless you installed it elsewhere as well. After the install is complete, you will see an output.

Now that you have *Forever* installed, you can start it:

```
forever start main.js
```

You'll get a notification saying it is processing the file *main.js*, which means you should be able to access the *app*. You'll also notice that you're outside of that instance in *Terminal*. So, if you were to close *Terminal* completely, the app would still function as normal.

This is an example of how you would deploy a *Meteor* application using *Apache 2*, and the *proxy pass module* in *Apache 2*, in order to serve the application through *Apache* and do some internal translations between the ports and the address.

This gives you an idea of how advanced *Apache 2* can get. You can do many other things. For instance, if you were using *WordPress* and wanted to enable a pretty *URL*, or *permalinks*, you would need a *mod* of rewrite module enabled:

```
sudo a2enmod rewrite
```

It would now be able to activate the new configuration. You just need to reload the *Apache2* servers using system control.

Installing and Configuring phpMyAdmin

Before we get started installing and configuring *phpMyAdmin*, let's talk about what it is. *phpMyAdmin* is a graphical interface for interacting with *MySQL* databases that you can use to access your browser.

You can find it in the official repositories of *Ubuntu*. It should be in all *Ubuntu* derivatives. **Open** *Terminal* and install *phpMyAdmin*:

```
sudo apt-get install phpmyadmin
```

Set the *MySQL* admin *password*. It then creates a configuration file.

Edit the *Apache 2* configuration file:

```
sudo nano /etc/apache/apache2.conf
```

At the bottom of this file, type **"Include /etc/phpmyadmin/ apache2.conf"**. Save, exist, and then restart *Apache 2*.

Take a Tour Around the phpMyAdmin Panel

If you open a web browser, you should be able to access and log in to the administrator panel. Type *localhost/ phpmyadmin*, and it should remember your password.

This should look familiar if you have used servers that use **C Panel** as the management tool.

You can create a new database here:

```
mydb
```

Let's create a user's table and have *4* rows. Name the rows *"ID"*, *"username"*, *"email"*, and *"password"*.

This is run-of-the-mill *phpMyAdmin* stuff, so I won't go into detail; but I will give you a heads up on a few things. You can browse tables and create a new table. Click over to the **Structure** tab to see the current columns or to add or delete columns. You can use *SQL*. You can search through the database, but I found that with *phpMy Admin*, search functionality is limited.

If you choose browse, you can browse the table's data. You can export the database, so if you're switching hosts or servers, for example, you may need to export your database. It will export the entire database in *SQL* format, *CSV*, or *PDF*. You have all of these options here. You can also import a database or table; just browse for the file that you want to import. You can also drop the table, rename it, and copy it. It is all pretty standard.

That's how to get set up with *phpMyAdmin* using an *Apache* web server on *Ubuntu*.

Creating a Basic Virtual Host

Let's create a virtual host. In a previous section you deployed the *Meteor* application and created a virtual host for it. This is a follow up to show you how a basic virtual host configuration would look. With the *Meteor* virtual host, we had to omit certain information that would normally be in a static website virtual host, and we had to add some things.

Open *Terminal* and change directory into the */html* directory. Create a new directory inside */html* called ***"site1"***, and then create another called ***"site2"***. If you run ***ls*** and list the directories, you will see that you now have sites *1* and *2*.

Add an *HTML* file to each of these:

```
nano ./site1/index.html
```

Then add some text:

```
This is my first site, located at
site1.localhost
```

Save and exit, and do the same for *site2*.

Go to your *Apache* directory, and create two files in the */sites-available* directory. You want to do this at the *sudo* level with administrator privileges:

```
sudo nano sites-available site1.conf
```

In the file, open *VirtualHost* at any web address on port *80*. This will listen and try to find the site you just created. The first thing you need is a server name, and this will act as the *URL* with the domain. So if you were going to point *example.com* to the server using the *IP* address of the server, the request reaches the server and then parses all these enabled websites to get further information about where the site is stored. Even if you are using modules, you can do that in a virtual host as well.

Set a **DocumentRoot** with an absolute path. In this case it's the */html* directory, and it's at the subdirectory called */site1*.

The file will look like this:

```
<VirtualHost *:80>

ServerName site1.localhost

DocumentRoot /var/www/html/site1

</VirtualHost>
```

Save and exit. Do the same for *site2*:

```
sudo nano ./sites-available/
site2.conf
```

It's the same syntax, except you will reference *site2* in the server name and the document root. This will be at */var/www/ html/site2*. Save and exit.

You need to go into the hosts file to create that internal route: *sudo nano hosts* in the */etc* directory. You'll see the *app.localhost* that you created earlier is still there. You will add *site1.localhost* and *site2.localhost*.

The hosts file on a *Linux* system is basically just a way to create your own records of redirection and to resolve different hosts by different domains are *URLs*.

Start the *Apache* service. You need to enable the site, so run ***"sudo a2ensite site1 site2"***. Restart the service:

```
systemstl restart apache2
```

If you open this in a web browser, you should be able to see the different routes in effect. Go to *http://site1.localhost* and you should see the first site. Then, if you go to *http:// site2.localhost*, you'll see the second virtual host site. If you go into *var/www/html*, you will see that you can have as many websites as your disk space permits, and you can serve up each at its own domain name.

And that's what a virtual host does.

Setting up a WordPress Installation on Top of Apache 2

To get started setting up *WordPress* on top of the *Apache 2* environment, you first need to grab the *WordPress.zip* file from *www.wordpress.org*. Then you'll extract it and place it into the */html* directory.

After the download of the *WordPress* installation files is complete, open the file manager. Go to **Downloads**, right-click the file, and extract it into the same folder. Copy the extracted files. Go to ***Computer/var/www/html*** and drop files in there.

Now you need to create a virtual host for the *WordPress* directory. **Open** *Terminal* and go into the *Apache 2* directory / ***sites-available***.

First, enable a module so the *WordPress* installation will be able to use pretty *URLs*, or *permalinks*:

```
sudo a2enmod rewrite
```

You'll receive a confirmation after it has been enabled.

Create the virtual host for the *WordPress* installation:

```
sudo nano wordpress.conf
```

Write to the file using the same syntax you used to create a virtual host before, but this time replacing the *ServerName* with *wordpress.localhost* and the *DocumentRoot* with */var/www/html/wordpress.*

Most of *Apache* uses *CamelCase*, by the way, so there should be a capital letter at the beginning of each word into a directive. Think of it like in programming when you set the variable. That's essentially what's going on here, except it's not called a variable; it's called a directive.

You need to configure some things using the directory. You'll configure the root directory first. Then, you'll configure the directory of the *WordPress* installation.

You do this by typing **<Directory /var/www/html/ wordpress>**. Now you can close that directory down. This is the basic configuration for *mod rewrite* in a virtual host:

Options Indexes FollowSymLinks MultiViews. Then type **AllowOverride All**, and then **Order allow, deny** and then type **allow from all**. This will make sure that *htaccess* file work in the rewriting. We'll have a look at the custom *htaccess* rewriting later. Here's what your file should look like:

```
<VirtualHost *:80>

ServerName wordpress.localhost

DocumentRoot /var/www/html/wordpress

<Directory / >

Options FollowSymLinks

AllowOverride All

</Directory>

<Directory /var/www/html/wordpress>

Options Indexes FollowSymLinks
MultiViews

AllowOverride All
```

```
Order allow,deny
```

```
allow from all
```

```
</Directory>
```

```
</VirtualHost>
```

Save and exit.

You also need to enable the site:

```
sudo a2ensite wordpress
```

Restart *Apache* using *systemctl*.

Let's edit the hosts file:

```
sudo nano hosts
```

Create another redirection internally to the system:

```
wordpress.localhost
```

Save and exit.

Set up the Database in WordPress

Before you can start setting up *WordPress*, you need to set up the database. Go to **localhost/phpmyadmin** and log in with your *username* and *password* that you created previously for *phpMyAdmin*. **Click New** to create a new database. Let's call it *"wp1"*. Click **Create**. That's all you need to do here.

For the *WordPress* installation, go through it graphically, and I'll show how you have to do it manually later. The database name is *wp1*. The *username* will be the same that you set up for the *MySQL* user. In this case it is *root*. Use the same *password* you set up for *MySQL*. Click **Submit**. If you get a message that the *wp-config.php* file can't be created, just copy the text in the field. We'll create the configuration file manually, and after that we can run the install.

Go into the */html* directory. You will see a sample configuration file. We'll look at that in a second. For now create a new configuration file: *wp-config.php*

Open the new configuration file with a text editor, and paste the text from the earlier window for the *.conf* file. Save and exit. Now you can go back and run the install.

Jerry Banfield & Nick Germaine

Add some information to the *Welcome* screen and click **Install WordPress**. Let's go log in at ***wordpress.localhost/ wp-admin***.

As you can see, you have a fully functional *WordPress* site installed on the *Apache* server. Let's make one configuration here. You can see if you visit the site, there's a really ugly *URL* when you click *"hello world."* Let's take care of that. In the admin site for *WordPress*, go to the dashboard in the settings for **Permalinks**. You can choose a different structure for the *URLs* here.

You'll note when you try to save the link structure, the directory is not rewritable by the server. You'll see some code that it tells you to copy. So, copy that.

The problem is that the server is running under the user *Apache 2* instead of your *user*, and the */html* directory is owned by the *user*. So, you need to change the *user Apache* is running to match your *user*, and then everything will be fine. The web server will be able to read and write all of these files. But right now it does not.

Let's create a new document called ***".htaccess"***. Open it with a text editor. Paste the code you copied from the links structure settings page. Save it. Now, you can refresh *Word*

Press. It should work, but if it doesn't, edit the code you just copied by removing the third line:

```
RewriteRule ^index\php$ - [L]
```

Now you have a working *WordPress* site. You can create pages and posts. From here, you would just work in *WordPress* as usual.

Python Installation and Command Line Interface

We're going to get started with *Python*. We will begin with basic installation, how to check your version, and a few things such as the command line interface Idol.

In *Ubuntu 15.10* and its derivatives, *Python* is preinstalled. There are two active versions in development by the *Python* guys. If you will be developing a new program, I usually recommend using *Python 3*. If you are jumping into an existing project that is already using *Python 2*, you would need *Python 2*. The differences between the two are very minimal, but they are code-breaking differences, so you can't just run a *Python 2* application using *Python three*. It won't work.

We will be using *Python 2* because we need to use a few modules. We will circle back to *Apache* because we will deploy a python application through *Apache* and make it accessible to the web.

First, in *Terminal*, check for the version of python that you have:

```
apt-cache policy python
```

For now, we are going to install *PIP*. I don't recall whether it is an acronym or an abbreviation, but it is basically *Python's* own package manager.

Let's install *PIP*:

```
sudo apt-get install python-pip
```

If you will be using *Python 3*, you will need to install *python3-pip3*.

We will use *PIP* to install python modules later, but for now I want to cover the python interpreter.

Python is an interpreted language, while *C* and *C++* are compiled languages. You wouldn't typically compile a *Python* application. You would actually use a real-time *CLI* interface program called *Idol*, and you can do that by just typing *"python"* in the *Terminal*.

To set a variable in *Python*, just type the name of the variable. For example:

>>> age = 300

>>> print age

And it prints: *300*

If you want to use a different version of the *Python* interpreter, you can exit, and then in *Terminal* type *"python3"*, and you will get the most recent version of *Python 3*. You can also type *"python3.3"*, and if you have that specific version, you can run that interpreter.

Python is installed and you are good to go. Next, we'll cover modules.

What are the Practical Applications of Python?

I want to talk about how truly powerful *Python* is and why it's so powerful. Many times, when I see people learning *Python*, they will get a handle on the syntax and the internal functions, and they wonder, well, how is this practical? What can I do with this? They are basically missing modules. Modules are the way that *Python* has been extended to be such a great environment for programming

We will look at one specific extension, or module, in *Python*. We will install it, begin using it, and we'll deploy the *Python* application through *Apache*.

In this section, you will begin using a module called **web.py**, which allows you to use *Python* to serve a web page.

First, let's install the module:

```
sudo pip install web.py
```

You'll see a progress bar and then a message that *web.py* has been successfully installed. We're going to start using *web.py*.

Let's set up a basic example of this *web.py*. We're going to look at how to import modules in *Python* using *"import web"*. Note that *GET* returns the class. And we will set the application variable and instantiate it. The first parameter is *URLs*, and it will take the routes we enter, then globals.

If you had multiple classes that you wanted to return multiple routes, add the second class, and then define the second class below. You could even load up an *HTML* template file from files, inject variables into the template *html* files, and then return that as a string. That's a more practical application, but we will not go into that here.

Open a text editor. *Python* requires four-space indentation. So, change your text editor to do four-space indentation if it is set to something else. Enter this into your text editor:

```
#!/usr/bin/python

import web

urls = (

'/', 'myClass',

'/about', 'secondClass'
```

```
)

class myClass

def GET(self):

return "<h1>Hello World</h1>"

class secondClass:

def GET (self):

return "<h1> This is the second
route</h1>

application = web.application(urls,
globals()).wsgifunc()|
```

Save into the */htmlL* directory in a new *Python* directory. You can call it */main.py*, and exit.

CHAPTER 9

Managing Users, Permissions, and Groups

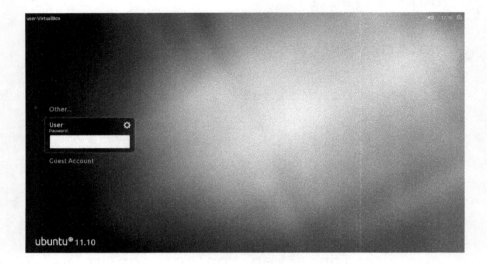

Adding/Removing Users Through Graphical Interface (GUI)

We are finished with development and moving on to more basic *Linux*. I say basic because now we will be looking at users. It's pretty simple stuff. It's important, but less commonly used.

We'll do this graphically and through command line. Let's do it graphically first so we can get that out of the way and move onto more fun stuff.

Open the system settings in *Ubuntu*. If you are using *Unity*, open dash and type *"system settings"* or *"settings"*. If you are on *Gnome* or any other desktop that uses a full-screen launcher with a search, it should be the same. If you are using a menu, you would usually find settings by going to **System Tools**. The system setting should look the same on most desktop environments that use *Gnome* components. I believe most desktop environments use *Gnome* components, including *GTK*.

If you are using *KDE* or any *KDE-based* desktop environment, the system settings application will look very different. Either way, you should have a user accounts item in the settings.

Click **user accounts**, and guess what? You can't do anything, because you have no authorization to do anything at the system level in this program. You need to unlock it. Click **Unlock** and enter your *Linux* password. Now, you can click the plus symbol and create a new user account.

Standard refers to a user with no access to *sudo*, and *administrator* would have access to *sudo*. For now, just create a *standard* account.

You can log out to the login manager or the display manager and log in as this user, or you could go into the command line and switch user. For now, let's learn how to delete user accounts. Highlight the user on the left and click the minus symbol. You'll be prompted whether you want to delete files or keep files. If you choose to delete files, this user's home directory will be removed. If you keep files, they will remain.

Let's get out of here and learn how to do this in *Terminal*.

Adding New Users Through Terminal

Bring up *Terminal*. You will use a program, or command, called *"adduser"*. Run this at the root:

```
sudo adduser username
```

The user will be added, along with a group for the user. You'll need to enter a user *password*. You can enter additional information, or just hit **Enter** through all of the following options, and finally type *"y"* for *yes* to end.

Now you have a new user account. Switch over to that user and take a look. Let's assume the username is *nick2*:

```
su nick2
```

After you enter the *password*, you'll see the user in *Terminal* at the prompt. It will also have the computer name and, if you are in any directory, that will be listed as well. Let's get *nick2* into the *sudo* account.

Switch back to your main account. To add *nick2* to the *sudo* file:

```
sudo adduser nick2 sudo
```

It's similar to adding a user, but there are two additional parameters. If you only added one parameter, it would assume you were just adding a user. When you add two parameters, it will add the first parameter to the second one as if it was adding user to a group. And that's exactly what this will do. This will add the *nick2* user to the *sudo* group so that *nick2* can use *sudo*. Now, you can switch back over to the *nick2* account to see what privileges this user has.

You'll see a message appear with instructions for logging in as *sudo* for the first time, so let's go ahead and use the command it gives you:

```
sudo touch textfile
```

It's working. Now, if you list the directory, you have *textfile* there.

And that's how you add user accounts in *Linux*.

Deleting Users Through Terminal

You've learned how to add and delete users in the graphic interface and how to add users through *Terminal*. Let's bring that full circle and delete users through *Terminal*. Let's delete the *nick2* user:

```
sudo deluser nick2
```

It's as simple as that. If you tried to log in as that user, it won't work. The user has been deleted.

How to Change an Existing User's Password

Once a user exists, it's pretty self-explanatory how you would change a user password through the *GUI*, so we'll focus on *Terminal*. The command in *Terminal* for password is ***"sudo passwd username"***. Next, you'll get a prompt, and you can change the password. Simple, yes?

Adding Users to a Group and Why It's Valuable

In this section we will learn how to create user groups and why you would want to do it. But first, let's talk about file permissions again. This is something we covered early on, but it is actually relevant to groups.

Let's work with a user called *nick2* again. You can go ahead and add this user as you did previously. And let's create a file called ***"text"*** and play with permissions.

Add the file:

```
touch text
```

Let's also make a new directory called **"groupstuff"**:

```
mkdir groupstuff
```

And move *"text"* into *groupstuff*:

```
mv text groupstuff
```

Change to the *groupstuff* directory. This will keep things organized. List the directories, and you will see three fields: *read/write*, *read/write*, and a third, *r--*. These permissions apply, from left to right, to *owner*, *group*, and *everyone else*.

Let's create the group in *~/groupstuff* called **"tt"**:

```
sudo groupadd tt
```

Let's change permissions for just the group of the text file:

```
sudo chown nick2:tt text
```

Now, the group has *read/write* permissions for that text file. Any user in this group would also have access. Let's add a user to the group:

```
sudo adduser nick3 tt
```

You can see why it would be useful to have groups. Rather than changing permissions for every user, you can create user groups and control permissions for the entire group.

CHAPTER 10

Linux Network Administration Tools

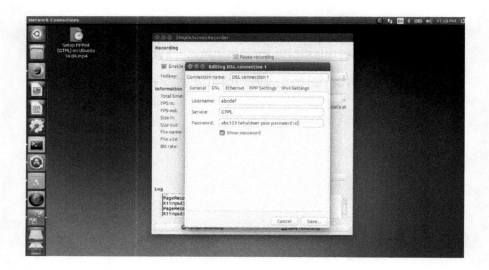

Introduction to Networking

We are moving on to networking. Networking is a big topic, so there is no humanly way possible I can teach you everything you need to know about networking. What I plan to do is give you the most essential and necessary information about networking, and then you can take that to further development. But this should be a good starting point for you. It should help you understand networks and what is

Jerry Banfield & Nick Germaine

happening on a network.

For a long time, I used the Internet before I actually understood what was happening. That may be the case with you too. I worked with an Internet service provider, but before that I thought the Internet was magic. You know, I opened a web browser, typed in a series of letters separated by a few dots and somehow, magically, it went out and found a web page. I didn't understand how, and quite frankly, I didn't care. This section will introduce you to some great information that I hope you can really absorb.

How Does the Internet Work?

We are going to talk about networking, specifically on *Linux*. You need to understand a few general concepts before we get to that, so, this is the introduction to networking in general.

If you are on a computerized device watching a video on the Internet, you are connected to a *router* or a *modem router* all-in-one device. The router is connected to your Internet service provider, and your Internet service provider has devices that are connected to the bigger world of the Internet. When you open a web browser, type in *Google*, and then hit

Enter, your web browser sends that as a request. It is basically saying, okay, this is the web page that this computer wants to see right now. It sends that request through your router, which sends it to your Internet service provider. Your Internet service provider has all of these fancy computers that properly route requests to *DNS* servers. A *DNS* server says okay, you gave me this string of text, a domain name or *URL*, and I have a record here that shows this domain or string of text should serve up content at this *IP* address.

The Internet does not understand *google.com* or *facebook.com*. The Internet uses network addresses. Think of it like each web server out there has an address, just like every house on your street has an address. If you were to send someone down the street to *Joe's Place*, you would say, go to this address. You would give them the address to *Joe's Place* and they would find it

The same thing happens on the *DNS* server. You get the *DNS* server and domain name, and the server says: I know this domain name should route to this *IP* address. Your request gets translated to an *IP* address, and other information, in order to go to the correct server. Then, the web server running *Apache*, or something else, receives the request and all of the related information, such as cookies, session variables, and the exact item you want to see.

If you go to *website.com/something/something else*, everything after the *.com/* is called a *URI*, which indicates the piece of content on the server you want to see. Think of the first part, *domain.com,* as the server with which you want to communicate, and then afterward, the place or page the server needs to go to retrieve the request you sent. The server does its rendering process and sends you that page in the exact same route that your request took to get there. It's similar to when you send your friend down the street to *Joe's Place* to pick up a box of pizza. Your friend walks down the street, turns left, then right, and he arrives at *Joe's Place*. He walks in and says, *"Hey, I need to get a pizza."* *Joe* gives him the pizza, and then he walks back the same way to your house. And before you know it, a web page has loaded in your computer box. That's how it happens.

What is a Local Network?

The Internet is technically an interconnected collection of networks. All of these little networks, all over the world, can now be connected to other networks in the world, and so we have the Internet. To understand a network, we need to bring it down from the top level to something more localized.

A local network is the type of network that you have set up in your house, where you connect to the *router*. The *router* can interact with the Internet for you, and then return the information to your computer.

Let's talk for a moment about *IP* addresses and the current issues that face them while we are still using *IPv4*. An *IP* address looks like this: *24.244.91.19*. This is probably someone's *IP* address, I don't know. If you typed it into a browser you would find out.

IP addresses can go from *1.1.1.1* to *255.255.255.255*. As you can imagine, the range is large, but it's not quite large enough for the human population. We've been running out of *IP* addressees for the last 15 or 20 years. Multiple solutions have tried to solve this problem. One of them was called *NAT*, a network address. You have one router, one *IP* address, given to you by the Internet service provider. With the use of a *router*, you can plug one device into the modem, and your computer will use this *IP* address in requests. When you send a request to *google.com* to load a page or to load a search, your *IP* address gets sent to *Google* as well so that *Google* can return this data to your device.

But what happens when you have one *IP* address and seven computers? That is when an *NAT* comes into play. This *IP* address is now the *IP* address of your *modem* or *router*, and it assigns *NAT* addresses to all the devices on your *network*. Let's say you have two devices on the network. The *IP* address of your router looks something like this: *192.168.0.1*

The *IP* addresses that your router will assign to computers in your home will begin with *192.168.* The IP address of your first computer may look something like *192.168.0.19.* Your second computer may be *192.168.0.20*, and your third may be *192.168.0.21.*

If you have three devices on your network, your router is keeping track of them through those three *IP* addresses. So, if you type *google.com* into the address bar using your first computer, the *IP* address for that computer and the request gets sent to the *router.* The router then sends the request off to the *ISP* and then over to the Internet, along with the *IP* address of the router. *Google* then sends the page back to the router *IP* address, and the router then connects it with the device that made the request. That is how a router interfaces between a local network and the Internet.

In the old days, before the *NAT* address and routers took off, each one of these devices would have had a different *IP* address. You would have had three *IP* addresses, but we found a way that you only need one for your network. The *IP* addresses you will see in *Terminal* are local; they are the three, or however many you have, that your router manages for your local devices.

One other special *IP* address is *127.0.0.1*. On every computer, this means this computer. It is basically a self-identifying *IP* address. If I put this special *IP* address into my browser, I would see my local host, whereas, if you put your special computer *IP* address into your browser, you would see your local host. The *NAT IP* address works basically the same way. If I typed one of my *NAT* addresses into the browser, it would try to find a computer on my network that has that *IP* address.

Practical Networking Commands

In this section we will look at some practical networking in *Terminal*. Open *Terminal*, and let's first talk about the ***"ping"*** command, what it means, and what it does.

You can ping an *IP* address or a domain name to see if you can get a successful response from it. If you are using a web browser and trying to troubleshoot whether or not the web browser is working, or whether your entire Internet connection is working, you may go into the command line and run the *ping* command on a known host that you know will always be up, for instance *google.com*.

Let's do that in *Terminal*:

```
ping google.com
```

You will get a response. You will see the length of time each response is taking to return to you. You'll also see other things, such as the exact *IP* address and the server that it is reaching. This will continue until you close it, so go ahead and exit. You get a breakdown of what happens on your network. You could let this run for a while to see if you were getting any packet loss through your network card. That is what pinging does.

Next, we will talk about the command ***"ifconfig"***. In command line on *Windows*, you have a command *ipconfig* that spits out a bunch of information about your network configuration. In *Linux*, the *ifconfig* command does the same thing. It will link to your *IP* addresses or network interfaces. In the first column of information, you'll see the name of the interface. For example, you may have an ethernet, and that will be listed here. You may see a *Local Loopback*, which is like a virtual interface, and it has your local host address. Next, you may have a wireless ethernet, which will probably show you are receiving bytes, if you have it running.

"RX" refers to what you receive. *"TX"* refers to what you transfer out. This will also show your *IP6* address and your *NAT* address. This may be useful to see if you are getting a valid *IP* address from the router, or to see if it's working at all.

Let's look at a command called *"tcpdump"*. It is a really powerful command line packet sniffer. It can analyze the packets that are going in and out of your computer network. First, you need to install it, if you don't already have it installed:

```
sudo apt-get install tcpdump
```

Run:

```
sudo tcpdump
```

This will also run until you cancel it. It's likely large and you can't capture all of it, so you can run a command to capture part of it. Let's capture *10* packets:

```
sudo tcpdump -c 10
```

You can analyze those captured packets to see where they are going and from where they are coming. The first column is a time stamp. You can see your *IP* addresses, your device, and that your device is sending packets out to your router.

You can also print the captured packets in *ASCII*:

```
sudo tcpdump -c 10 -A
```

You can use this if you are trying to see what is coming in and going out. If you want to listen on only one network interface, run *"ifconfig"* again, with the name of a device:

```
sudo tcpdump -c -i wlo1
```

The *"-i"* tells it to listen to the interface that follows in the command line.

You can also display them in *hex* and *ASCII*. This may make sense if you are looking for some *hex* response from these packets:

```
sudo tcpdump -XX -i wlo1
```

You can also capture packets from specific ports:

```
sudo tcpdump -i wlo1 port 22
```

The *tcpdump* command is good for troubleshooting network activity.

Using the netstat Command to Track Detailed Network Statistics

We're going to talk about a command called ***"netstat"***, which is an abbreviation for network statistics. Based on the flags you pass to *netstat*, it will return different statistics.

The ***"-n"*** option makes netstat print addresses as dots, or dotted *IP* addresses, rather than symbolic host network names. This will make sense if you want to see the actual *IP* addresses rather than the domains that are connected to the machine. Run it like this:

```
netstat -nr
```

It returns information regarding the *IP* routing table. The *"r"* flag in that command states that you are looking for the kernel *IP* routing table, which shows how things are routed.

Let's display network interface statistics using the *"-i"* command:

```
netstat -i
```

This shows the usage of each of your devices. For example, you can compare the bytes sent and received from your local host or your wireless interface.

You can display connections to your machine using *"-ta"*. This will look for active sockets and print out the status, such as foreign addresses connected to the local address. If you run *"netstat -tan"*, it will display *IP* addresses instead of host names.

This is useful because you can combine elements of the different flags that you are passing to the *netstat* command,

and the display changes according to how each of these outputs work. This is how you would use *netstat* to view active connections and active routes of *IP* addresses internally through command line. If you think your computer may be connecting to a malicious host, you can take these *IP* addresses that you find and look them up through a website like *www.network-tools.com*.

An In-depth Look at the Linux Hosts File

First, we'll look at the hosts file in terms of local host. We touched on that briefly when deploying the *Meteor* app with *Apache 2*. You went into your hosts file to create some routes for the app.

The hosts file is in */etc/hosts*. Go ahead and open that:

```
sudo nano /etc/hosts
```

If you've been following along, you'll see what we set up in here earlier for *app.localhost, subdomain.localhost*, and *python.localhost*. I didn't really explain earlier to what extent you can use this file.

As I explained in the network introduction, the *DNS* server holds records of what domains point to what *IP* addresses. Think of this hosts file as an internal *DNS* lookup functionality. When you go to *app.localhost*, your computer first checks the hosts file. If it doesn't find an entry for a domain in the hosts file, it goes out to the *router*, and then your *ISP*, and then a *DNS* server. By adding entries here, you can override default behavior of known domains that you want to change.

Choose an *IP* address. You can get this *IP* address for any site at *www.network-tools.com*. Once you get the *IP* address and copy it, type it in a browser to see the page it returns. This is the page to which you want to route. Jump back to the hosts file. This file can take three columns, and we've only discussed two so far. Let's cover all of the columns here in greater detail

The first one is the *IP* address to where you want to route. The second column is the domain for the host name to where you want to route. The third column is an alias. For this example, use the alias *"go."* Add the *IP* address you just copied to the first column. Add *go.com* to the second. Save this file, and go to your browser and type: *go.com*

You're just setting *DNS* records for this machine. You could create shortcuts for your favorite websites, with the exception of *Google*, because Google has a lot of internal routing. Sometimes this will work; sometimes it will not. It depends on how the web server is set up. Usually, I just use the hosts file to set domains to go to my local host. I usually use this when I'm developing something that needs to have a *URL*. In *WordPress* configuration, you could configure a domain and then point it to your local host.

Now, let's talk about your host name. A host name is basically the name of the machine. You will see this host name in *Terminal*. You can use the host name similar to how you use custom hosts. For example, you could have your computer name route to your *Apache* default page. You can also update the host name, but first you need to do a few other things.

Let's set up a host name and name it *"Megazord"*:

```
sudo host namectl set-hostname megazord
```

You need to edit the hosts file to update the host name there as well. Open the hosts file, and replace the current name of your machine with *Megazord*. Save and close the hosts file, and then restart:

```
sudo service hostname restart
```

The host name is now set to *Megazord*. If you were to relaunch the browser and type in *http://megazord*, it would indeed return the default *Apache 2* page.

Using traceroute to Track the Servers a Request Passes Through

Let's look at the traceroute command and install it:

```
sudo apt-get install traceroute
```

When installation is complete, you can run it, followed by the domain you want to trace:

```
traceroute google.com
```

It will spit out every server the request jumps through in order to reach *Google's* server. When you see *three asterisks*, that means the request has timed out on that server, so it will try another one.

You can trace the servers with which you're communicating as you try to reach *google.com*. When you type google.com into your browser, it doesn't just go from your router straight to the *Google* servers. There are many intermediary servers between the two, including your *ISP*, the *DNS* servers, and other servers that need to be hopped in order to get to *Google*. And this is what you're seeing with this command. You'll see the *IP* address of your *router* and the length of time it took to get there. Next, you'll see the address where it goes from there, and each address following. You will actually see it hopping to different addresses around the world. The host name will show, if it is available, and you'll see the *IP* address in brackets.

Let's try this with your own server:

```
traceroute yourservername.com
```

You will see your *ISP* and your virtual private server provider. You can track your server stops.

Using Network Mapper to Track the Activity on Your Network

I want to give you one more tool to help you with networking on *Linux*. Let me introduce you to *"nmap"*, which is an abbreviation for network mapper. It is an open source tool that can tell you what devices are on the network, what *IP* addresses are in use, and what services each machine is offering.

Install nmap:

```
sudo apt-get install nmap
```

The first thing we will cover is how to scan specific *IP* addresses. You can get your *IP* address by typing this in *Terminal*:

```
ifconfig
```

Copy your *IP* address and run it with *nmap*. For example:

```
nmap 192.168.0.100
```

You can see what ports are available, their status, and the service they provide by name. You should have *Apache* installed on your machine. If you went through the section on *Apache*, you'll see the same thing here. The port is *80*, and the status is open because you have it running. It runs automatically on startup. The service the port provides is *http*. If you were also running an *SSH* server on your machine, you would see another entry in this list for port *22*. It would show the status as open and the service as *SSH*, or something to that effect.

If you want more information:

```
nmap -v 192.168.0.100
```

In this command, *"-v"* stands for *verbose*. Verbose mode, in most applications, aside from the regular output, also gives you more direction on what's happening in the application. It provides more information than you would normally get. In this instance, it may be running more scans. It scans the *IP* address for all ports, and it finds all of the ports that are open and closed.

You can scan multiple *IP* addresses in a variety of ways. First, let's specify each address, separated by a comma for

Jerry Banfield & Nick Germaine

the last values of the *IP* address:

```
nmap 192.168.0.100, 1,2,3
```

You can also scan a range of *IP* addresses: *192.168.0.1-100*

The more you have, the longer it takes to scan. When we talked about *IP* addresses, we discovered that you can use anything from *0* to *255*. So, if you want to scan all *IP* addresses that begin with *192.168.0*, you could use:

```
nmap 192.168.0.0-255
```

Or you could use a wildcard:

```
nmap 192.168.0.*
```

Setting Up a Networks File for Network Mapper

With *Network Mapper*, you cannot only scan devices on your local network, you can also scan external *IP* addresses or host names. You can create a file of networks that you want to scan regularly, whether on your own network or an external. This can save you time, if you have several networks that you want to scan frequently.

Try scanning the host name for your server. Here's an example of mine:

```
nmap pointybracket.net
```

If you have many open ports running, it could take a while to scan. This will tell you the number of ports closed and list the open ports.

Let's create a file for scanning networks. First, open a text editor and a new document. In the open text file, list the host names and the *IP* addresses you want to scan. Mine looks like this:

```
pointybracket.net

192.168.0.1

192.168.0.100
```

Save and close it. Save it as *networks.txt*.

Back in *Terminal*, give a command to scan the hosts in that *networks.txt* file. Be sure to tell it where the host is located. It returns in the order they were scanned. Here's an example:

```
nmap -iL ~/networks.txt
```

You can turn on *OS* detection during the scan, which tells you which *OS* versions are running on the devices on the network:

```
nmap   -A 192.168.0.0-100
```

You can also scan to find out which devices are up and running using the flag *"-sP"*. You can find out why a port is in a particular state by using the flag *"--reason"*. You can choose to show host interfaces for a machine using *"--iflist"* in the list of arguments for this command. There are many more map commands you can use. Just do a *Google* search to find out more options.

One reason you may want to run these commands is if you notice the Internet is running slowly in your home. Let's say you have *10* people in your house and only some of them are online. You could run network mapping to find out how many people are online and what devices they are using. Or, you could find the *IP* address for a device that you may need to use to access a certain service on another machine.

CHAPTER 11

Setting Up a SSH Host on Your Local

Using SSH to Access the Command Line of a Remote Host

What is *SSH*? It's the abbreviation for *Secure Shell*. It allows you to access the *shell* or command line of a remote host that has an *SSH* server set up.

In a previous chapter, you connected via *SSH* to your own server. We're going to do that again and look at this process in more detail.

To connect to a remote host through command line, use **"ssh"** and the connection string. You will enter the username on your remote host:

```
ssh nick@pointybracket.net
```

You can use the domain name of the host, any other domain that points to the host, or the *IP* address. You will be asked for your password for the remote machine. You could then run the **ls** command on any directory on that remote machine and take a look at the files. Once you get connected, all of the commands are the same, because it's basically just a remote *Linux* shell. When you are finished, just type *"exit"* and the connection will be closed.

Use SFTP to Transfer Files To and From Machines

Before we look at *SSTP*, let's answer a similar, but different question: What is *FTP*? *FTP* is an acronym for *File Transfer Protocol*. It uses port *21* to transfer files between two machines. In regular *FTP*, everything is transferred in clear text, so if anyone is sniffing packets on your network, like you learned in a previous chapter, they would be able to read all of those packets. For this reason, I recommend never using *FTP*.

SFTP is easier anyway, and that's what we are going to use. Similar to the *ssh* command, you would use *"sftp"* and then the connection string.

You will be connected to the remote host. You can list files on the remote machine with **ls**, but we also have a few different commands to list what's on the local host, while connected to a remote host. In this case, if you run **ls**, you list the files on the remote machine. To list files on your local host, run the **"lls"** command.

Now you can transfer files back and forth between the two machines. If you want to move, or push, a file called *text.txt* from your local host to the remote machine, it will transfer with the same file name: *put text.txt*

Now you can run **ls** on the remote machine and see that file.

In a similar way, you would use the **"get"** command to pull that file from the remote machine to your local host: *get text.txt*

Then you can run **lls** to see that file has indeed been moved back to your local machine.

Setting Up an SSH Host on a local Machine

It's actually quite simple to set up an *SSH* host on your machine. You'll do this using *Terminal*. First, you need to install **"openssh-server"**, so go ahead and run *apt-get* to install the program. By now, you're an expert at installing programs on *Linux*.

Once you've installed *SSH*, you're going to make it more secure by making some changes to the port configuration and authentication so that no one will be able to log in as *root* user. You will also add a list of approved users and restrict all others from logging in via *SSH*.

Run the configuration file:

```
sudo nano /etc/ssh/sshd_config
```

Change the port from *22* to *2212*. Scroll down and under authentication, change permit root login to **"no"**. Scroll down again, and add a line at the bottom: *AllowUsers youruser*

Save the file and close it. Now you need to restart *ssh*
service.

I'm going to explain a concept you can do with *ssh* that will
remind you of the movie *"Inception"*. In order for this to work,
this would have to be the only machine on your router, or you
would have to set up, through the router, *DMOZ* port
forwarding for port *2122*.

Let's say I *ssh nick@pointybracket.net* and then *ssh* into
my local machine. This allows me to connect from an external
host to my local host. When I go to the *IP* address of my
server, it goes directly to my server. It's not configured through
NAT addresses. My server actually has five *IP* addresses, and
those *IP* addresses go directly to my server. And that's why I
can access *SSH* on that server without having to configure
any routers or anything.

Using the man Command to Learn Info About Programs on Your Linux Machine

The *"man"* command helps you discover all the different
flags you can use for different programs, as well as different
options that you can pass for those flags. You can also use

man to get general information about a program.

In *Terminal*, you use *"man"* followed by the program you want to search. For example, if you wanted to learn more about the *SSH* command, you type **"man ssh"**, and this will show a manual page about the *SSH* program. It shows a description of *SSH* and then detailed descriptions of the flags and options you can pass to the command.

You use **"q"** to quit the *man* command.

You could use the *man* command on *chromium-browser.* I use this example because there are many options for launching *chromium-browser.* Many times people ask for help, and the help is right there on the computer, but they don't know where to find it. The *man* command will help you find much of the information you need to work in *Linux* command line. This is one of the best forms of assistance you can get for *Ubuntu* or any other *Linux* distribution that has *man* installed.

CONCLUSION

I want to take the opportunity to congratulate you on taking your first step toward becoming a *Linux* power user. I'm honored to share my knowledge about *Ubuntu Linux* with you and to help you take that first step toward becoming a *Linux* master.

If you are considering going into *Linux* administration, I hope this is the stepping-stone that propels you even deeper into *Linux*. There is a lot more to learn about *Linux*. We've only scratched the surface. Thanks for joining me in this learning experience.

If you want to learn more about *Ubuntu Linux*, you might also be interested to take my online course **"Ubuntu Linux: Go from Beginner to Power User"** which has already served *5,000+* students.

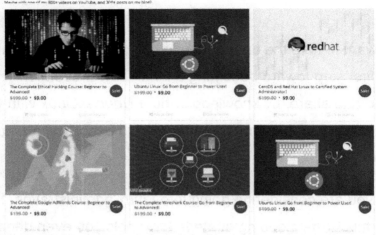

<u>START LEARNING NOW</u>

https://jerrybanfield.com/product/ubuntu-linux/

You can read more books written by me at *https:// jerrybanfield.com/books.*

I appreciate the time you spent reading this! If it has been helpful for you, I hope you will let others know that in a review at *http://jerry.tips/kindle01sp*

Jerry Banfield

https://jerrybanfield.com

LEGAL NOTICE

www.ingramcontent.com/pod-product-compliance
Lightning Source LLC
Chambersburg PA
CBHW071420050326
40689CB00010B/1918

* 9 7 8 1 5 3 5 3 2 5 2 6 4 *